Tell Us a Story

JULIUS FISCHBACH

Broadman Press • Nashville, Tennessee

© Copyright 1978 • Broadman Press.

4236–15

ISBN: 0–8054–3615–4

Unless otherwise noted, all Scripture quotations are taken from the Revised Standard Version of the Bible.

All Scripture quotations marked KJV are taken from the King James Version

Dewey Decimal Classification: 252.53

Subject Headings: CHILDREN'S SERMONS//CHILDREN'S STORIES

Library of Congress Catalog Card Number: 77–87251

Printed in the United States of America

Preface

"Tell us a story" is a familiar request in every language and in all nations around the world. No one knows when it was first voiced, but the time was probably in the Sumerian or Babylonian period of history. Certainly it was popular among the Greeks, the Romans, and the Hebrews.

A story suggests children, but the child in each of us continues to enjoy facts presented in story form. When the whole family worships together in a church service and the children are recognized with an appropriate story, the entire congregation benefits.

It has been my practice during a long ministry to include the boys and girls in every service, being careful to choose for the junior sermon an illustration of the main theme of the worship program. Though retired from full-time service in the ministry, I have continued in interim work and have continued to include the children in the church program. About five years ago Dr. Wallace Robertson, former senior pastor of Peoples Church, East Lansing, Michigan, asked me to serve as associate minister on his staff. This position gave me opportunity to preach once a month and to talk to the children when they are included in the worship service.

The children of Peoples Church, of course, are the reason for this book of stories. They are an interesting group: alert, eager, and multi-talented. They are vocalists, dramatists, artists, game enthusiasts—and much more. Furthermore, they are a multitude in number and truly an inspiration.

More about the stories. My wife, Mildred, shared her good judgment in the selection of themes; and she listened to the first drafts of the stories. Our grandson, David Julius Heater, read a number of them and gave his approval. Many of them have been told to the children of our church, and they responded favorably.

The final copying of the manuscript was done by three good friends who are artists with a typewriter: Paula (Mrs. Dean) Telder, who assumed the main responsibility, and her assistants Fran (Mrs. Wallace) Piper and Lorna (Mrs. Rowland) Baker. I am deeply grateful to each and all who contributed to this project and feel that it would not have been possible without their timely and capable assistance.

JULIUS FISCHBACH

CONTENTS

Great Personalities

1.   Neil Walked on the Moon
NEIL ARMSTRONG

One thing I do, forgetting what lies behind and straining forward to what lies ahead, I press on toward the goal (Phil. 3:13).

Neil cannot remember when he was not interested in flying. As a small boy he used to dream that he was hovering in the air. Then, when he woke up, he continued to day dream about going up in a plane. He was more interested in making model planes than in playing baseball, football, or hockey. He did join the Boy Scouts, and he played baritone in a four-boy jazz combo for a while; but flying was his hobby.

He read everything he could find on the subject and would go to the airport and watch the planes take off and land whenever he could get his parents to take him. His father, an auditor for the state of Ohio, traveled from county to county and often took his family with him. Neil lived in many different places when he was small, but he always managed to find the airport and watch the airplanes.

When he was six years old Neil took his first ride in an airplane. When he was fourteen he took his first lesson in piloting a plane. This required more money than he received from his allowance, so he worked afternoons after school in a drugstore to make the money. He did so well in his flying lessons that he got his pilot's license on his sixteenth birthday.

Neil's parents had taught him to work hard, to save his money, and to always be thankful to God. He learned these lessons well and has practiced them ever since. He has always believed in doing whatever he does to the very best of his ability. He was also taught that education is very important, and he worked hard at school. After completing high school, he enrolled at Purdue University. Of course, he majored in aeronautical engineering. He was also registered as a Navy cadet.

After just two years in College, he was called to active service in the United States Navy as an aviator and sent to Korea. Again he worked hard. He flew seventy-eight missions and won three Air medals. When he was dismissed from the service, he went back to Purdue and earned his bachelor's degree in science.

When Neil left college he could not think of doing any kind of work that did not involve flying. He became a test pilot and flew all kinds of experimental planes. It was dangerous work. He flew supersonics, rocket planes, and all sorts of new models. Some of these planes flew at speeds of four thousand miles an hour, and some went to altitudes as high as forty miles. He was in this dangerous business eight years.

Then Neil joined the Air Force and was assigned to the Space Project. That was where he got his big opportunity. He was part of the team that docked a spacecraft, but his greatest exploit was going to the moon. With two other astronauts, he went to the moon in the Apollo II spacecraft. Two of the astronauts landed on the moon's surface in their landing module called the Eagle on July 21, 1969. Neil was the first to go down the ladder from the Eagle and put his foot on the surface of the moon. As he did, he uttered the words that are now engraved on the pages of history: "That's one small step for man, one giant leap for mankind."

Yes, Neil's last name is Armstrong; and he was the first man in the history of the human race to walk on the moon. Edwin "Buzz" Aldrin followed him a few minutes later and probably many more will do the same in time; but Neil was the *first*.

When we read Neil Armstrong's philosophy or the motto he lives by, we think of the apostle Paul's words: "One thing I do, forgetting what lies behind and straining forward to what lies ahead, I press on toward the goal" (Phil. 3:13). He believed in giving all he had and doing his best. Neil Armstrong put it this way: "The single thing which makes any man happiest is the realization that he has worked up to the limit of his ability, his capacity. It's all the better, of course, if this work has made a contribution to knowledge or toward moving the human race a little farther forward."

12

2. How Many Lives?
DR. ALBERT SCHWEITZER

For whoever would save his life will lose it; and whoever loses his life for my sake and the gospel's will save it (Mark 8:35).

Our question is: How many lives can one person have? That may seem to be a curious kind of question, but we really mean to ask it seriously. We think of a person's life as lined up around one profession or special work for which he is known. For instance, when we say the name Beethoven, we think music. When we say Shakespeare, we think theater; Raphael, painting; Edison, inventions. Usually the majority of a person's time is taken up with the one important thing that he does and for which he is famous—if he does it better than others.

There are some great men who have been equally famous for more than one achievement. We are thinking of Dr. Albert Schweitzer, who died in Africa, where he was serving as a missionary doctor. Before becoming a doctor and a missionary, Dr. Schweitzer had already made a name for himself and had become famous in four other fields. He was internationally known both as philosopher and theologian. He was also a successful author of books on theology and music. He was a world authority on the music of Bach and was a concert organist. He played in the great cathedrals of Europe. Not only did he play the organ, but he also built organs.

So it seems reasonable to say that Dr. Schweitzer had successfully lived four lives before he became a missionary doctor. Then he lived another successful life in Africa, working with sick patients in his Lambarene hospital.

But those five lives were not all he had. No one could count the lives Dr. Schweitzer influenced. Hundreds of young people went on to do great deeds because Dr. Schweitzer inspired them with his own dedication and zeal. Some of these built other hospitals; some entered the ministry; some became teachers; some went home to be better husbands, wives, and parents. All who met him were better for having been in his presence. Of course you cannot say that Dr. Schweitzer lived the lives of those whom he influenced, but he did have some part in their living—some bearing on their lives. They would never have made the decision to do their special work if they had not met the great doctor. When you try to add up all the good he did—well, you just can't!

How did such a great man come to be in the first place? As a boy at school, Dr. Schweitzer noticed the poor clothing of many of the other children. His conscience would not allow him to wear the good warm clothes his parents had bought for him. He could not wear a fine woolen overcoat when many of the boys in his class had no overcoat at all. He could not even eat the nourishing food his parents served when he knew many of his friends had only mush and water. So very early in life he did some deep thinking. When he became twenty-one he said to himself: "I cannot accept my comfortable way of life and take it for granted. I must do something to pay back the benefits I have received."

He took seriously the words of Jesus, "Whoever would save his life will lose it; and whoever loses his life for my sake and the gospel's will save it" (Mark 8:35). He decided to continue in his four professions until he was thirty years old. Then he would try to find out, by making a survey, what the most needy section in the world was. He would then ask, what do these people need most of all: food, education, medical care, or some other evidence of care? He found this place to be French Equatorial Africa, and the greatest need was for a medical doctor.

So Dr. Schweitzer went back to school and started at the beginning to learn the science of medicine and surgical skill. He received a thorough medical education. Then he went to Lambarene, Africa, built a hospital there, and spent the rest of his life helping the people of that African region. No one can possibly estimate the good he did.

So we ask again, as we did in the beginning, just how many lives can one person really have?

3. Jane Wanted a Big House

JANE ADDAMS

I heard the voice of the Lord saying, "Whom shall I send, and who will go for us?" Then I said, "Here am I! Send me!" (Isa. 6:8).

God is constantly calling people to do the important work he needs done in the world. He calls boys and girls to prepare for the jobs he has for them when they grow up. God's voice is not *heard* when he makes this call, but the person has a feeling deep down that recognizes a need that somebody should take care of. There is also a conviction that that someone is you.

A long time ago, in the city of Chicago, there was a girl by the name of Jane. Her last name was Addams, spelled with two *d*'s. Jane's father was the owner and operator of two mills. One was a sawmill where people sawed logs into boards, and the other was a gristmill where people ground wheat into flour and corn into meal. Jane very much wanted to visit the mills and see how they worked. One day her father took her along with him when he went to his office.

Jane was thrilled with the machinery in the mills. She watched the logs move toward the big whirling saw and the boards come out at the other end. She watched the big round stone wheel grind the grain in the gristmill. She played with the wheat in the bins and with the sawdust from the sawmill. But all the time she was playing, she could not get her mind off what she had seen on the way to the mills. The streets were very narrow, and the homes were just shanties. And the boys and girls! They were dirty. They were playing in the narrow streets, and they did not even have toys to play with. The boys were batting a tin can around with sticks, and the girls were making mud pies in a dirty mudhole.

Jane could not understand all of this. She went to the office and asked her father many questions. Why were those children playing in the street instead of on the playground? Why were they wearing such ragged clothes? Why did they use tin cans and mud instead of balls, dolls, and toys? Her father told her there were no playgrounds in that part of the city. The children had no toys; they had to make their own games. Their parents did not have the money to buy them

15

good clothes and warm jackets to play in.

Jane could not go back to play with the wheat and the sawdust. She kept thinking about those poor boys and girls. She said to herself: *When I grow up I will have a big house with a big yard. I will invite all the children to come and play in my yard and stay for lunch in my house.*

It took a long time for Jane to work out her big idea. She went to school and to college and studied sociology (which is all about people and how they live) and economics (which is all about how people make their living) and other subjects. In fact, she studied both in America and in Europe.

In 1889 Jane found just the big house she wanted on Halsted Street in Chicago. It had been the home of Mr. Charles Hull, an early citizen who had died. This house was a large one and had once been a very fine building in a prosperous section of the city. Now the neighborhood was a slum, and poor people lived there. But Mr. Hull's house was just what Jane was looking for. She called it Hull House and lived there the rest of her life. She did just what she had dreamed about doing as a little girl—and much more. She made a home for all the children in the neighborhood. She also taught them to want better things in life and helped them to become better.

Jane taught their parents, too. She determined to make things different in the city itself. A born reformer, she worked to make the city a better place in which to live. She worked against child labor and slum neighborhoods. She gave lectures and wrote books. In fact, she accomplished so much that she was given the Nobel Peace Prize along with Dr. Nicholas Murray Butler, president of Columbia University.

Of even greater importance, she helped thousands of poor families to have a better life and thousands of boys and girls to be happy and grow up to be useful men and women. Best of all, she won the praise of the Master, who said: "As you did it to one of the least of these my brethren, you did it to me" (Matt. 25:40).

4. Free to Worship—or Not

ROGER WILLIAMS

There is one lawgiver and judge, he who is able to save and to destroy (Jas. 4:12).

The very moment the Johnson family climbed into the car on the church parking lot, everyone started talking at once. "Boy, I was really scared when that policeman came down the aisle," said Jane.

"It didn't scare me a bit," said Joel. "I knew it was some kind of gag."

"Yes, but it really was not a 'gag' as you call it," said their mother. "It was a very serious lesson to teach us an important fact in our national history."

So the conversation went on and on, and very briskly, too. Everyone wanted to tell how he felt when the surprise visitor came down the aisle—and what he thought about the whole affair. You see, that morning in the church service Reverend Woodley slowly approached the pulpit and said: "Today I am Roger Williams. The time is 1635, and the place is the church in Salem, Massachusetts. Hear what I have to say to you. Things have been happening in this town and in this colony that are contrary to the will of God. As all of us are witnesses, our fellow citizens have been shamefully treated. They have been put in the pillory and in the stocks and exposed to public ridicule for no other reason than their failure to attend services at the church on Sunday. This is absolutely evil and must stop! The police have no right to judge anyone on his or her religious practices.

"There are other evils being practiced in our country, and I will continue to defy them until they are stopped. The very idea of the King of England giving property in America to persons, villages, or colonies is absolutely dishonest. It amounts to plain robbery. This land does not belong to him or to England. It belongs to the Indians who were here when the white man came to these shores."

Reverend Woodley was actually shouting, which was quite different from the way he usually preached. Right then was when it happened. Reverend Woodley had just spoken about robbing the Indians when a policeman walked down the middle aisle of the church and stopped directly in front of the pulpit. He held up his hand and commanded the preacher to be silent. Then he unrolled a paper and began to read:

"Hear ye, hear ye, all men! The High Council of the Commonwealth of Salem, Colony of Massachusetts, judges one Roger Williams guilty of willful declarations and accusations unlawfully made against this High Council of said Commonwealth and hereby condemns the same Roger Williams to be banished from the colony of Massachusetts from this time forth and for evermore."

Then the policeman demanded that Reverend Woodley come down from the pulpit. He led the preacher up the aisle and out of the church, while all the congregation sat in shocked silence.

In a very short time, perhaps one minute, Reverend Woodley returned to the pulpit through the door at the back and proceeded to explain the meaning of what had happened. He said it was a dramatization of an actual event in the Salem church in the year 1635 when Roger Williams, pastor of the church, was officially banished from the colony of Massachusetts. The cause was his public statements against the authorities. They were arresting and punishing people because they had failed to attend church on Sunday. Roger Williams' only crime was that he objected to this practice and made a public protest from his pulpit in the Salem church. He insisted that public officials could judge people only on matters of civil disorder—not religious matters. Then Reverend Woodley preached a Bicentennial sermon on religious liberty and insisted that it was one of the most important provisions in our Constitution.

He also told the congregation that when Roger Williams was banished, he was befriended by the Indians. Shortly afterward he bought a tract of land from them and established the town of Providence. He called it Providence because he felt he had been providentially saved from cold and starvation. For the constitution of his new community he wrote a statement of absolute freedom of religion as the main provision. This was the first community in the world to be founded on the principle of liberty of conscience.

The Johnson family agreed that this had been a church service and a sermon never to be forgotten. Joel said it in one sentence: "That sermon was a WOW!"

18

5. The Man Who Stopped Fights
DR. RALPH BUNCHE

Blessed are the peacemakers, for they shall be called sons of God (Matt. 5:9).

When someone does such an unusual job that he receives world recognition, we like to find out about him. Where was he born? What was he like as a child? What kind of education did he get? Was he a friendly person or a grouch? Did he have a sense of humor? What kind of games did he play—baseball, football, tennis? Was he a swimmer, a jogger, a skier? Did he ride a bike? Was he a good neighbor? Did he act "high hat," or was he a good fellow?

Dr. Ralph Bunche would come out well in answers to all these questions. He was what we might call a "regular guy" and was well liked by all who knew him. He was born in Detroit, Michigan, and was the grandson of a slave. He lost both his mother and father when he was twelve years old. His grandmother took him to her home after this tragedy. She taught him to be considerate of others and always to do his very best when given a job. He never forgot her teaching.

Dr. Bunche worked hard all his life. When in grade school he delivered newspapers and ran errands. During his high school days he worked after school, yet he was a good student and was graduated from Jefferson High School in Los Angeles with the best grades in his class. Then he went to the University of Southern California and worked his way through by serving as a janitor and by laying carpets. He must have worked the clock around, for he was graduated with the highest honors (summa cum laude and Phi Beta Kappa). In addition to being a scholar and a worker, he was an athlete. He played both baseball and football and was the star guard on three championship basketball teams.

He wanted to get all the education he could, so he went to Harvard University and got his Ph.D. degree. Usually students working for a doctoral degree read a lot of books and take a lot of notes. Ralph Bunche did his work differently. He was concerned about people in the poor nations of the world—especially in Africa. So he went to West Africa and lived there for many months. He traveled around in a native truck, asking questions and making observations. He wanted to know if the people of Africa were able to govern themselves and if they were mistreated when controlled as colonies by European countries.

Dr. Bunche became a professor at Howard University and later at Harvard University. He also was a secretary in the United States Department of State. But his fame came when he became Secretary of the United Nations and was sent to Israel to settle the dispute between the Arabs and the Jews. That was where he earned the title "Peacemaker." His job was so difficult that some said it was impossible, but he succeeded in ending the war between the Arabs and Israel by arranging an armistice.

As one newspaper explained it, Dr. Bunche became "instantly famous" because of his great success in this armistice. *The Saturday Evening Post* came out with an article carrying the headline 'The Man Who Stops Fights." Most of the papers and national magazines praised him for his success. He was given honorary degrees by twenty different colleges and universities, and he received forty medals and awards. But the greatest recognition he received was the Nobel Peace Prize for being the man who did more in that year than anyone else in contributing to the cause of world peace. Dr. Bunche was the first Negro in history to receive the Nobel Peace Prize. With all his honors and recognitions he remained a modest, humble person.

How did he succeed in doing what was considered so difficult an undertaking? One factor was his determination to do all within his power to bring about peace. He was told that this would be a slow job and that it would take a long time. He said, "I am here to do this job, and I will stay here until it is accomplished if it takes ten years."

Another thing was his quiet, steady, firm way of tackling the job. His private secretary said of him, "I never at any time saw him lose his temper." I suppose he did many times feel like flying off the handle, but when this happened he would stop for a while and play Ping-Pong or pool or just relax. Yes, Dr. Bunche was truly a man of goodwill, a true peacemaker. He always approached his fellowmen with open hands of welcome and kindness. To him, dealing with people of other lands meant an opportunity to make new friends and widen the circle of understanding and brotherhood.

6. George Makes a Discovery
GEORGE WASHINGTON

I planted, Apollos watered, but God gave the growth (1 Cor. 3:6).

Men and women who are doing important things in the world got started in the direction of helpful service when they were children—at least many of them did. God wants boys and girls to think about things that need to be done for him and begin training now for the big jobs later on. As we read the biographies of people who have been very useful by helping others and by serving as leaders in the community, we find anecdotes that show they began thinking of that kind of work very early in life.

One of these persons was George, and his last name—you guessed it—was Washington. George was called the "father of his country." You have heard many stories about George Washington: the time he cut down the cherry tree, the time he threw a dollar across the Potomac River, the time he climbed to the top of Natural Bridge (a great wall of solid rock). These stories may be true, and they may not be. No one knows for sure. And the story we are going to tell is in the same class. It is in line with the kinds of things he did later in life.

One day when George was eight years old, he came running excitedly into the house. He called to his father and mother, "Come quick and see what I found in the garden!"

Of course they followed him into the garden, and there he pointed out what he had discovered. In big letters, in living clover, was his name spelled out: G-E-O-R-G-E W-A-S-H-I-N-G-T-O-N.

They all looked at it in admiration, and his father asked, "George, do you think that just came up by itself?"

George had not really thought about it until then. "Of course it did not grow without somebody planting it. You must have planted it, Daddy!"

"Yes," said his father, "your mother wanted to give you a nice surprise. So I spaded the ground, and she planted the seed to spell your name. But that was not all. We could not make the clover grow. We just planted the seed. There was more to it than that."

21

"Yes, I know," said George. "God did the growing. So it took you and Mother and God, all three, and you did it just for me!"

George learned that day that God works with us to make plants grow and to make our lives happy and useful. George never forgot the lesson. All his life he was a man of faith and trusted in God as he made his plans and did his work day after day.

You probably have seen many pictures of different events in Washington's life. Have you seen the one of Washington kneeling in prayer at Valley Forge? It is said that that picture tells a true story. A soldier saw the general bowing in prayer and ran to tell his fellow soldiers. He reported "Everything is going to be all right, men; General Washington is praying." And things did turn out all right. We do not know what the general was praying about, but he certainly was concerned about his men who were cold and hungry and suffering terribly that winter day.

George was doing what he had developed the habit of doing: taking his problems to God. He knew that God cares about his children and their needs. He also knew that after we have done all we can, such as planting seeds, making plans, and working hard, it is God who adds the most important part of all and determines the outcome.

7. Angel with a Lantern
FLORENCE NIGHTINGALE

I was sick and you visited me (Matt. 25:36).

Were you ever in the hospital? I don't mean visiting a friend, but sick and in a hospital bed. If you were, you know how wonderful it was to have a nurse—in fact, several of them—come and take care of you. They knew just what to do, and they did it so gently and so well that you were always happy to see them. Nurses not only love people and want to be helpful, but they have studied and trained to know how to do their work well. Nurses today talk about a nurse of long ago who set the high standards of good nursing by her own unselfish life of helpfulness. She was Florence Nightingale. Her story is a thrilling tale of adventure.

Not a great deal is known of her early life. She was named for the city in which she was born, Florence, Italy, where her parents were living at the time of her birth. We can assume that in childhood she did the usual things that children do, but we can also imagine that she was especially interested in treating the sick and injured— dolls, dogs, cats, and other pets. From early childhood she had a real concern for living things suffering from any kind of injury or disease, and she wanted to do all she could to help them.

Her parents were well-to-do, and she was given a good education and enjoyed a great deal of travel. She could have lived a life of sheltered comfort, but that was not for Florence. She wanted to be where trouble was, and right in the midst of it, to do what she could to minister to need. After her formal education she took a regular course of training in nursing and also studied in hospitals in Paris and in Kaiserswerth, Germany.

When she was thirty-three years old, England and France were at war with Russia in that peninsula known as the Crimea, extending into the Black Sea. Florence learned that thousands of wounded English soldiers were suffering in barracks and makeshift hospital buildings, neglected and dying for lack of proper medical care. The British Secretary of War asked Florence to take a corps of nurses to the Crimea to correct this situation. She accepted the assignment and went with thirty-eight nurses. She and her efficient nurses did amazing things. They cleaned up the unsanitary buildings, introduced system and order into the care of patients, and by their scientific approach and constant attention saved hundreds of lives and made life happier for all the patients.

Florence was so concerned about the wounded soldiers that she personally attended them and went from bed to bed at all hours of the day and night. During the dark hours she carried a lantern and became known as the "angel with a lantern." Although her strict rules were resented at first by some of the attendants, she soon proved that her system was best. In time she was not only accepted but admired and loved by all. She contracted Crimean fever and nearly died. Her friends urged her to give up her strenuous work and go home, but she determined to stay, saying, "I can endure anything the men can take."

Florence was not satisfied with completing this job. She made a study of hospitals in many places and found better ways of conducting care of the sick. She wrote many books on hospital management and care and was recognized as a world authority on the subject. She was given the Order of Merit by Queen Victoria and received many other honors, but she was not willing to rest on her laurels. When she was given $150,000 by her admiring friends, she used the money to build a home for nurses in London. Although she eventually became a semi-invalid, she continued to carry on her work through letters and writing. Many famous people visited her with their problems, asking her advice. She continued to be concerned about sick and needy people around the world.

No wonder Florence Nightingale is held in such high regard not only by nurses, but by all who know about her wonderful career of service. She proved what great good one person could do in a humble profession if that person were truly dedicated to the task and thought of it as a work to be performed in the sight of God to the very best of one's ability. She made nursing a profession of great honor and high privilege.

8. Queen of the Gospel Song
MAHALIA JACKSON

Sing to the Lord, bless his name; tell of his salvation from day to day (Ps. 96:2).

This is the story of a person who has sung the praises of God all her life. Mahalia Jackson was born in a shack on Water Street in New Orleans. Her family practiced their religion, and singing gospel songs came as naturally as eating and sleeping. The family was very poor; and, as a child, Mahalia never had a Christmas tree or a doll. But she did have love. Her father combined manual labor and barbering with preaching. All week he worked with his hands, and on Sunday he preached the gospel. Mahalia did her first singing at home, but her first public singing was in the church where her father preached. That was a fine team: daughter singing, father preaching.

Mahalia's parents did not want her to listen to jazz or popular music. For the most part she heard only sacred selections and hymns. She sometimes visited friends in their homes and heard other kinds of music, but she preferred to hear and to sing gospel songs. In later years, when she became popular as a singer, she had many invitations to sing blues songs and jazz in nightclubs and in the theater, but she refused them. She felt that that was not her kind of singing.

Mahalia's mother died when she was only six years old, and Mahalia had to leave school shortly afterward and help earn money to support the family. She worked as a laundress and maid. She worked hard and always did her work well. People liked her, and she had no trouble getting a job. But she wanted to sing.

When she was sixteen she went to Chicago to study beauty culture. While studying, she worked as a chambermaid in a hotel. But always on Sunday she was in church, singing in the choir. She was also a member of a quintet that traveled to various churches to give music programs. After she completed her beauty culture course she opened her own beauty shop in Chicago, but she continued to sing at every opportunity.

She made her first record in 1934. In 1945 a record she made of a song, "Move On Up a Little Higher," became a hit and sold a million copies. This got her started on her singing career. She was invited to sing in Carnegie Hall in New York City. (She has sung there a dozen times since.) This high honor was followed by a concert tour of Europe. She sang in England, France, Denmark, Holland, Germany, and Switzerland. She made a special trip to the Holy Land, where she visited the garden of Gethsemane and Calvary and lived over again the passion of her Lord.

When she started on her European tour, she was given a bon voyage party in Washington. Many persons high in government circles were there to greet her. While abroad, she was welcomed by Queen Elizabeth and Sir Winston Churchill when she sang in Albert Hall in London and by Sigward Munk, mayor of Copenhagen, when she was in Denmark.

Mahalia has more invitations than she can possibly fill. She has been invited to sing for many prominent persons. She sang for President Eisenhower on his birthday in 1959 and was on the program for the inauguration of President Kennedy in 1961. She has also sung at many national rallies and patriotic occasions. She often donates her time for charity programs. She appeals to groups of all ages; and the halls are filled to capacity, with standing room only, whenever it is announced that she will sing.

Mahalia's singing is quite different from the singing of other vocalists. She does not sing to entertain but to share her religious experience and convictions with her audience. She lives every song she sings. She puts all of herself into her music: her hands, her body, her eyes, her face, her voice. The range of her voice is amazing. She sings high falsetto tones that are like sweet whispers, and she drops down to low notes that are like bass tones. She never sings a song twice the same way because she sings it just as she feels at the time. Though it is different, it is always a living testimony of her faith and her love for her Lord.

Mahalia usually starts her program with the song "My Home Over There." The words speak of finishing the Lord's work here and "walking the golden stairs" to the "home over there." Mahalia says, "I believe that one day I shall do that."

9. The Man Who Taught the World to Read
DR. FRANK LAUBACH

Go therefore and make disciples of all nations . . . . teaching them (Matt. 28: 19–20).

Think of giving an order to a publisher for 300,000,000 copies of books and study materials. Furthermore, consider that these materials must be printed in a dozen different languages, with drawings and illustrations. That is just a hint of the kind of big business Dr. Frank Laubach was engaged in as he determined to complete his job of teaching the whole world to read.

But the story began a long time ago. When Frank Laubach finished his studies at Princeton University and went to work on his Ph.D. at Columbia University, he was concerned about the millions of people in need around the world. He wrote his doctoral thesis on the problems of city slums, and he learned about them firsthand as he worked at Spring Street Settlement House in New York City. When he received his Ph.D. degree he was not satisfied with framing it and hanging it for display on his living room wall. He accepted an assignment from the American Board of Foreign Missions to do mission work in the Philippines. Why the Philippines? Because he was determined to give his efforts toward solving problems in one of the most difficult spots in the world. For this reason he went to a particular island in the Philippines, to a particular tribe of people, the Moro in Lanao.

The Moro were a fierce people, and Lanao was a dangerous place for anyone to go. Dr. Laubach wanted to share the Christian religion with these people, who were Mohammedans and very hostile to Christianity. There was another problem as great or greater than their hostility and their ferocity: The great majority of the Moro were illiterate. Dr. Laubach felt that he could not get very far with his missionary work until he taught the people to read, but how could such a tremendous task be handled?

First of all Dr. Laubach learned their language—Maranaw. This language, though spoken by all the people, had never been reduced to writing. There was neither printing nor longhand of any kind. So after learning to speak Maranaw, he set to work to develop letters

27

and words to spell out the language. Then he tackled the more difficult task of teaching illiterate people to read their own language.

How would you even start such a seemingly impossible undertaking? Dr. Laubach made his beginning by asking some of the educated people to make a list of a number of key words—words used by common people every day. Then he made charts with letters representing certain sounds. This is called *phonetics*, and he hit upon an idea that proved to be almost miraculous. He found he could make charts representing basic sounds and symbols by which he could teach illiterates to read in a very short time. In fact, some bright pupils learned in half an hour. Some actually got the basic idea in fifteen minutes.

We might find an illustration to help us understand the phonetic principle by its use in some systems of shorthand. Some shorthand writing is abbreviation of words, but some systems use symbols to represent sounds. When the sound system is used, a person who is expert in using it could take dictation in a different language. Even if he did not understand the meaning of the words, he could read back the sounds.

Dr. Laubach was so successful in teaching the Moro to read with his symbol charts that learning became a popular endeavor with them. It seemed that everyone wanted to learn. They had great gatherings where they were taught in groups as well as individually. Dr. Laubach and his helpers (for he had to call in leaders to handle the great numbers of learners) went from place to place, answering the invitations to teach. There were celebrations following these teaching schools. Learning to read became a leading interest with thousands of people.

So many wanted to learn that more teachers were needed than could be supplied. Then came a great idea. It was suggested that each one who had learned the principle of the charts would teach someone else. So the slogan took hold: "Each-one-teach-one." Then this movement really snowballed.

Dr. Laubach was invited to India to use his method of charts to teach the illiterate there. Teaching reading and writing was more difficult in India, for there are so many dialects and the language is not phonetic as is that of the Moro. However, with the help of educators who supplied key words and assisted with the charts, the work was accomplished; and millions more who were illiterate learned to read.

28

New ideas were introduced from time to time. Two very important ideas were the addition of pictures along with the symbols and the idea of connecting one picture with the next to aid memorizing.

It is impossible to tell the complete story here, but the movement went from country to country. Dr. Laubach found that languages could be reduced to symbols and charts and that reading could be taught simply and quickly to any person who really wanted to learn.

Practically all the countries of the world have been included in this great literacy program: Asia, Africa, and the islands of the sea, as well as Central and South America. No accurate count of the number of people who have been included could be made. When each-one-teach-one moves into action, there is no end to the possibilities of the outreach.

Dr. Frank Laubach, the kindly man of goodwill who loved everyone everywhere and taught the world to read, died in 1970 at the age of eighty-six; but his great work continues to go forward. It will never stop until the entire world is able to read and, as Dr. Laubach insisted, hopefully reading the best literature—especially the Bible with its message of God's love, hope, brotherhood, and peace for all mankind.

10. She Found the Priceless Pearl
MARIE CURIE

The kingdom of heaven is like a merchant in search of fine pearls, who, on finding one pearl of great value, went and sold all that he had and bought it (Matt. 13: 45–46).

A pearl can be anything that is valuable. A "pearl of great value" could be a rare substance not only costly to produce, but also of great usefulness to mankind. Such a substance is radium. A woman, with the help of her husband, discovered this miracle element. Manja or Marie Sklodowska was her name, but we know her today as Madame Curie. She was born in Warsaw, Poland. Her father was a high school teacher of physics, and her mother conducted a school of her own for girls. Marie was a very bright child and learned to read when she was only four years old. Learning came easy for her. She had a prodigious memory. She enjoyed reading so much that her mother had to urge her to "run out in the yard and play." She would much rather have read a book or done arithmetic problems just for fun. There are not many boys and girls like that, but her love for learning prepared her for the important work she was to do later on.

In school the Polish boys and girls had a real problem. Russia ruled Poland and required that the Russian language be used in the schools. The Polish language was forbidden. However, Polish families were very proud of their history and wanted their children to learn both the language and the history of Poland. Marie and her schoolmates did speak Polish and studied Polish traditions and history, but they had to do it undercover. Their teachers helped them in this, but whenever the Russian inspector came around they had to hide their Polish books and speak in Russian. It was really dangerous to be caught with Polish books.

Marie had problems all through the years, but she managed to handle them well. Her mother had tuberculosis and would not even kiss or hug her children for fear of giving them the disease. She died when Marie was eleven years old. The family was poor; and when she was eighteen Marie worked as a governess to help pay the bills. However, she wanted to get a good education, and she continued to study. She

30

went to the university in Paris (the Sorbonne) and lived in a garret. Day after day she had only bread, butter, and tea to eat; but she made the best grades in her classes. She was determined to become a scientist and to do research work, so she studied late into the night.

Marie received her degree in science from the Sorbonne and married a professor of physics, Pierre Curie. Both she and her husband were interested in finding out all about radioactive materials. They experimented with various substances and found that a great deal of radiation came from a substance called pitchblende. This was a very expensive ore, but they decided they could work with the ashes or residue of the ore after it was used to make glass. They made arrangements with a manufacturer to buy the used ore and started the big job of melting out the radioactive substance from the pitchblende.

Their first problem was acquiring a place to work. The only workshop they could find was an old shed on the campus, which was a terrible place to work. It was cold in the winter and extremely hot in the summer. The roof leaked, but the shed was the best spot they could find. So they had some pitchblende hauled to the shed and started work.

Marie did most of the hard manual labor as well as measuring and testing. Her work was mainly in the courtyard. She boiled down the pitchblende in large vats with the heat in her face and the smoke in her eyes. She did the monotonous chore of putting in more and more of the ore, taking out the residue or ashes, and sorting out the tiny bits that were radioactive from each batch.

It was a terribly tedious job: the same tiring work, hour after hour, day after day, week after week. Actually, she melted down eight tons of the pitchblende. It took four long years to get enough of the miracle substance to submit to the test. Finally the long job was finished, and one-tenth of one gram of the pure metal was produced. It was a new element not known to scientists before this time. They were thrilled beyond expression. For the first time in the world a mite of very radioactive substance had actually been produced. The Curies had discovered and captured the pearl of great value. Marie and her husband went to the old shack at night to see this miracle substance glowing in the dark. They named it radium.

Of course, many things happened because of this great accomplishment. Marie and her husband were given the Nobel Prize in Science and received recognition from kings and heads of state. Radium could be used to treat cancer and other diseases and in industry. In fact, no one knew how wide its use might be and how important it might become.

A tragedy happened about this time. Dr. Pierre Curie was killed in an accident. His death was a terrible blow to Marie, but she continued to carry on her scientific work. She bore her sorrow heroically. She also carried her great honors with humility. She continued to be a sincere, hardworking, kindly person, just as she had always been. Success did not go to her head, for she had no desire to make personal profit from her achievement. She gladly gave her discovery as a gift to the people of the world.

From the Bible

11. A Captive Maid

Would that my lord were with the prophet who is in Samaria! He would cure him of his leprosy (2 Kings 5:3).

In the Old Testament we read of many cruel practices that were taken for granted because times were quite different from today. One of these was making slaves of persons taken captive in war. Our story is about a little girl from Samaria who had been stolen from her parents in a raid by soldiers and carried as a captive to Syria. Her captor gave her to his wife to be her servant.

We might expect this little girl to be very resentful toward her mistress and perhaps stubborn and determined to do as little as possible. She was just the opposite. She accepted her lot as a servant, kept a beautiful spirit, and worked hard to make her mistress happy.

One day she noticed that her mistress was sobbing and she asked her what the matter was. She found that her mistress' husband, the soldier who had captured her and made her a slave, was a very sick man. He was a leper. Leprosy is a terrible disease, and in those days there was no known cure. Naaman, the sick man, was the commander of the Syrian army. He was liked by all who knew him, and the king himself was his friend.

The little girl was very concerned, and she believed she knew a man who could cure her master. She told her mistress: "There is a prophet in my country who can make your husband well. Please have him go to Samaria and get help."

In those days, as in our day, people would do almost anything if they thought it would cure their disease. So Naaman took a number of his men and started immediately for Samaria. He also took a letter from the king of Syria to the king of Israel, asking that he receive Naaman and heal his disease. As was the custom in those days, he also took presents for the king of Israel: "ten talents of silver and six thousand shekels of gold, and ten suits of Festal Garments (2 Kings 5:5).

It was natural for both Naaman and Ben-hadad, the king of Syria, to suppose that the king of Israel was the man with power to heal diseases. That person was not the king, but the prophet Elisha. So when the king of Israel read the letter from the king of Syria, he thought this was some kind of trap to get him into trouble. Of course he was not able to heal diseases. The king of Israel was really frightened.

However, the prophet Elisha found out about the matter and sent his servant to the king's palace. He explained that he was the man they really wanted and directed Naaman to go and dip seven times in the Jordan River to be healed of his leprosy. Although Naaman had come all this way just to be cured of his terrible disease, he refused to bathe in the Jordan River. He said: "In my own country there are rivers that are clear and fresh, and the Jordan is a muddy stream. Why should I bathe in it?" In a huff he turned around and started for home. His servant reasoned with him, saying: "If the prophet had asked you to do something difficult, you would have done it. This is a simple thing; why don't you try what he has asked you to do?"

The story concludes in a happy vein, for Naaman decided to go to the Jordan River and bathe there. As he did so his leprosy left him, and he was healed. This caused him to be so excited that he declared, "Surely there is only one true God, and he is in Israel!" Then he did a peculiar thing. He had his servants dig up as much dirt as a donkey could carry, saying that he wanted to take it back to his country and use it as an altar for praying to the God of Elisha. He erroneously thought that Elisha's God could be worshiped only on Israel's soil.

The Bible tells us no more about the servant girl, but we can easily believe that her master and mistress were so delighted over Naaman's cure that they took her back to her home. There must have been great rejoicing over her safe return, and she probably "lived happily ever after."

12. The Boy and the Giant

You come to me with a sword and with a spear and with a javelin; but I come to you in the name of the Lord of hosts (1 Sam. 17:45).

My name is David. I am a shepherd and a shepherd's son. I live in a time when and in a country where there is much fighting and much killing. Bands of rough, armed fighting men go about the country and take what they want by force and bloodshed. To protect our country and our farms and fields, we must often fight these rough men. My three brothers are in the king's army, and they know what it is to face enemy armies and to fight to the death.

I know something about fighting too, but my fighting is against wild animals. Where I watch over my father's sheep there are wolves, jackals, and sometimes bears, leopards, and even lions. It is a shepherd's business to protect his sheep. I have stood my ground many times against growling wild animals, protecting the sheep that were crowded together, trembling with fear. The worst time to protect a flock is at night in the dark of the moon. When the moon is full you can see almost as well as in the daytime, but when the moon is dark wild animals can sneak up close and you do not see them until the light of your campfire reflects in their eyes. Then you sometimes have to fight them with your bare hands. This is tough work; but I know what it takes, for I have had to do it many times. Once I choked a bear with my hands, and on another night I killed a lion. Boy, was that a battle for me! God was with me, and I won.

A shepherd has a lot of free time, and I have spent much of it practicing with my slingshot. I aim at a rock on a stump or at a hole in a dead tree. I have done it so many times that I can almost always hit the target right in the center. The fact is, there have been times when if I had not been a good shot I would not be here to tell this story. It was a lion or a bear or me. But I do not give myself all the credit. I believe in God, and I know that God protects me. He also guides my hand and makes it possible for me to hit the mark when I am protecting my sheep.

But I want to tell the story of my fight with a giant: I mean a

37

giant man, not a beast. This fellow was terribly big. They said he was eleven feet tall, but I will explain that later. First let me tell the reason for my fight with him. My father told me to take some food to my three brothers who were in the king's army and also to take some gifts to their captain. When I arrived I heard a loud voice using the worst kind of swear words and calling our people dirty names. I listened for a while; then I asked some of the soldiers standing nearby what it was all about. They told me the story. The Philistines were fighting against our army. They had this giant, this eleven-foot fellow, and he wanted to make the fight a one–against-one affair. He said he would fight any man our army sent out, and the battle's outcome would be decided according to who won. What I could not understand was why our men were so afraid of that oversized bully. He was big, I admit; but the funny thing about it was that he must have been more afraid than anybody else. You know what? He wore tons of heavy armor. He was so covered up with brass and iron that he could only see out from a little peephole in front of his face. But that was not all. Listen to this: Besides his heavy armor covering him from head to foot and his big spear and sword, he also had a man going in front of him carrying a big shield to protect him. Was he something! He was a whole armored fort all by himself. He clanked and rattled like a pile of metal when he walked. In fact, I don't see how he could even walk, he was so stacked up with hardware.

When I heard that fellow yelling insults at our army, I decided to take him on myself and teach him some manners. My brothers thought I was crazy and wanted me to go back home. The king believed in me, though, and wanted me to wear his suit of armor. I had never had that sort of thing on in my life. I tried it on, but it made me feel as awkward as a scarecrow. I took it off. I wanted plenty of freedom to swing my arms and legs and shoulders. So I started out to meet this so-called champion.

First I stopped by the brook and picked up five smooth, round stones and put them in my shepherd's bag. I tested my sling to see that it was OK and started down the hill. When the giant saw me coming he called me all kinds of vile names and swore he would give my body to be eaten by the birds. Since he was so cocksure I said, "The same to you"; but I did not feel that I was able to tackle him by myself. I knew only God could handle this situation, and I told him so. I said, "I come to you in the name of the Lord of hosts" (1 Sam. 17:45).

Well, the battle did not last very long. It took only one rock. The Lord sent that rock right to Goliath's forehead (it was the only spot that was not covered with iron or brass). And, believe it or not, that big overgrown coward crumpled up and fell forward right toward me. I had to dodge to get out of the way. When he hit the ground the vibrations felt like a small earthquake. You should have seen his army, the Philistines, take to their heels when they saw him tumble. You really couldn't see them for dust!

There is a lot more to this story, but the rest is not important. The king wanted to see me. He told me I had saved the army and the country, and he said a lot of nice things about me. The women sang songs about me and about what I had done; but, really, I didn't do it at all. God was just using my arm and my sling, and it didn't take but about twenty minutes to finish the job.

13. The Boy Prophet

And Samuel grew, and the Lord was with him and let none of his words fall to the ground (1 Sam. 3:19).

As we read the Bible we realize that a person does not need to be old, or even grown-up, to be used of God. Many times a boy or a girl was God's messenger or minister. And in at least one case, a small boy was chosen to be God's prophet. The story of Samuel begins before he was born—and that, too, is rather unusual for a story.

Hannah was an unhappy woman because she had no children. In Old Testament days it was almost a disgrace for a married woman not to have children. Hannah went to the temple at Shiloh each year with her husband to worship and to sacrifice, and she always prayed that she might have a child. With her prayer she made a promise to God: If she were given a son she would dedicate him to God, and he should live in God's house all his life.

God answered Hannah's prayer and she was faithful to her promise. She named her son Samuel, which means "heard of God." True to her promise, she brought him to the temple and left him there with Eli the priest as soon as he was old enough to be away from his mother. This must have been hard for Hannah to do, but she knew Samuel would be well cared for; and she would come to visit him from time to time. Each time she came she brought him new clothes, and she probably spent much of her time at home sewing these garments and making them the very best.

We might wonder how a small boy could be useful around a church or temple. Of course, he could wait on the priest, bringing him a drink, acting as a messenger, or taking things to other priest's in the building. He could sweep up and keep the priest's quarters tidy. At any rate, Eli seemed to think a lot of little Samuel and found him good company.

We should add that Eli was an old man who had difficulty getting around. He probably used a cane. No doubt Samuel helped him to get settled in his chair with his scrolls, parchments, pen, and whatever he needed for his study and his work. There were several other priests working in the temple. In fact, Eli's two sons were also priests. They were supposed to help him and to serve all who came to worship there. But these two sons were bad men, not at all the kind of persons who should be serving in the temple. They were doing harm and not good. People who came to the temple to worship were offended by them and wondered why they were allowed to continue as priests.

Now Eli knew that his sons were bad men. He had talked with them and asked them to change their ways. But he was old and did little more than lecture to them. He allowed them to continue to serve as priests when they should have been expelled from the temple service.

The first prophecy of little Samuel was connected with these bad sons of Eli. Samuel was awakened from his sleep one night, and he thought Eli had called him. He went to Eli's room, but Eli said he had not called him and told him to go back to bed. Samuel did this, but twice more he thought Eli had called him. Then Eli realized that God was calling the boy and he told Samuel to listen to what God wanted him to do.

This is the way the small boy Samuel became a prophet. As he lay on his bed he heard God call and said, "Speak, for thy servant hears" (1 Sam. 3:10). Then the Lord told him that he was to tell Eli the bad news that he was to lose his priesthood because he knew his sons were evil and yet had allowed them to remain as priests.

Samuel loved old Eli and did not want to hurt him, so he waited as long as he could to tell him the bad news. When Eli called him and asked him to report the message God had given to him, Samuel bravely told him every word. Though Eli was saddened by the message, he realized it was God's word and said, "It is the Lord; let him do what seems good to him" (1 Sam. 3:18).

Samuel grew to be a wise and good man. He became an honored prophet and was one of Israel's truly great leaders.

14. The Little Daughter

Do not fear; only believe, and she shall be well. Child, arise (Luke 8:50–54).

One of the most popular stories in the New Testament is the incident of the raising of a little girl who was the daughter of a church leader. The name of the little girl is not given, but we know a good deal about her father. His name was Jairus; and he was the moderator or president of his church congregation, which was called a synagogue (the Jewish name). He was a loving father, as can be seen in his concern for his daughter and his reference to her as "my little daughter." He was also a brave man and a man of faith. The leaders of his Jewish religion frowned upon Jesus because he did not conform to their ideas. He had not attended a seminary to study for the ministry; he was not an ordained minister; and he was not recommended by the high priest. It took courage for Jairus to come to Jesus, for in doing so he was breaking the rules of his church. He came because of his belief that Jesus could heal his daughter and because he loved his daughter very much.

Jairus' faith was very strong. He said to Jesus, "My little daughter is at the point of death. Come and lay your hands on her, so that she may be made well, and live." One account says the little girl was dead; and two other accounts say that while they were on the way to the house, messengers came reporting that the girl had died and that there was no need of troubling Jesus since all hope was now gone. But Jairus did not give up hope, and Jesus rewarded his faith by going with him to his home.

This journey of Jesus to the home of the little girl shows the great love that Jesus had for all people, especially children. There was a large crowd of people waiting to hear Jesus preach, but he took the time to go to Jairus' house to minister to this girl in her need. This was an emergency. He could speak to the people later.

When Jesus arrived at Jairus' house there was a large crowd of neighbors there, crying and sobbing because they thought the little girl was dead. It was the custom in those days for families to employ professional mourners when death came to their homes and it would

42

appear from the Bible account that several of these persons were there making a noise as though in terrible grief. It was truly a sorrowful situation.

Jesus changed everything. He would not talk of death. He said, "Do not weep; for she is not dead but sleeping" (Luke 3:52). He ordered everyone to leave except the father and mother and three of his disciples. Then he went into the room where the little girl was lying on her bed, took her by the hand, and said, "Child, arise" (Luke 3:54). Then, Scripture records, "Her spirit returned, and she got up at once; and he directed that something should be given her to eat" (Luke 8:55).

How we wish the writers of the Scriptures had told us more. They tell us only that the girl was twelve years of age. What was the color of her hair? Was it curly? Did she have dimples? Was she the kind of girl who liked to help her mother around the house? Did she play a musical instrument? Did she sing? Could she draw or paint pictures? Did she like to play outdoor games? Did she swim, or jump rope, or play hopscotch? Did she go to a summer camp? What kind of student was she? Did she study hard and make good grades at school? Did she ever wonder what she might be when she grew up? Did she have a chum she liked to be with every day or maybe two or three special friends? Was she the kind of person everyone in the neighborhood liked? We are told that she was an only child. Was she badly spoiled, or was she thoughtful, kind, and helpful? These are only a few of the questions that might be asked. What do you think?

15. Hidden Treasure

The kingdom of heaven is like treasure hidden in a field, which a man found and covered up; then in his joy he goes and sells all that he has and buys that field (Matt. 13:44).

Most of us like to read about buried treasure or about fabulous stories of gold and silver known to be in a sunken ship somewhere in the South Seas or about a chest of valuable coins hidden by pirates in a cave on some mythical island. Interestingly enough, Jesus, evidently realizing how eager people are to hear about hidden treasures, told the story of a man who found a great treasure in a field. Not wanting anyone else to know his secret and to be sure he himself had possession of it, he bought the whole field and then, at his leisure, dug up the treasure.

Actually, I happen to know where this priceless treasure is. It is a secret, but Jesus gives us clues to the location. He calls the treasure the "kingdom of heaven" or the "kingdom of God"—and just think of the treasure included in that phrase! The very best of everything we have ever known could be wrapped up in those terms. But where is that kingdom located?

Again, we are dealing with an open secret, for when the Pharisees came to Jesus and asked about the kingdom, he said, "The kingdom of God cometh not with observation: Neither shall they say, Lo here! or, lo there! for, behold, the kingdom of God is within you" (Luke 17:20–21, KJV).

That is an amazing statement and points to a very important truth. When we are looking for the best things to happen to us, we will not find the answers in some distant place; nor can we secure them from someone else. The place to look is within, and the persons to give the answers are ourselves.

Many years ago a Philadelphia preacher, Dr. Russell Conwell, went about the country giving a most popular lecture. He called it "Acres of Diamonds," and he was invited to deliver it in churches, schoolhouses, and public halls in cities and villages all over America—and, I presume, in cities across the seas as well. It was a very simple story, and the gist of it was this: A man very much desired wealth and determined to search until he found it, no matter how far he must travel. So he started out looking, seeking, inquiring, asking, and traveling from city to city, going farther and farther from home until he had traveled around the globe. With all his effort and determination he failed in locating the riches he longed for. Then one day, discouraged, old, and tired from his endless search, he came back home and there—in his old hometown (and, as I remember, actually in his own backyard) he saw the most fabulous diamond mines in the world—the Kimberley diamond mines. Dr. Conwell then elaborated on his theme by relating story after story of people he knew who had made successes of their lives by discovering and developing some talent or some latent resource in themselves or in their own backyard.

But that is not just a story; nor is the truth of the story confined to the distant past or to some place on the other side of the globe. The treasure is still hidden, but it is right "here" waiting to be discovered; and the open secret is still the same. The greatest treasure in the world for you is right within yourself, waiting for you to uncover it and develop it to the limit of its potential.

What that treasure is no one knows but God and you; and perhaps I should say only God knows, for you may not realize what the treasure is that you possess, hidden deep within. It may be a talent for music—instrumental or vocal. It may be an ability to draw or paint or sculpt. It may be an unusual talent bent toward writing—journalism, fiction, biography, or history. It may be a natural skill for teaching or eloquence in public speaking. It could be any one of a thousand special aptitudes that you can discover, develop, and use for the good of those around you. Your own satisfaction in knowing that you are making a contribution and helping others will be boundless.

16. The Big Happening

There is a lad here who has five barley loaves and two fish (John 6:9).

Dan liked to fish. Well, most boys do. Dan liked to fish more than he liked to play games—any games. He had a fishing buddy, Matt, who was just as good a fisherman. But on the day when the *big thing* happened, Matt was busy helping at home and could not go along. So Dan took off for his favorite fishing spot all alone. A fellow does not like to give away the secret of his special fishing hole, and we will not say exactly where this one was except that it was somewhere on the north shore of the Sea of Galilee and was marked by a white rock that looked like a camel. You might not think it looked exactly like a camel, but both Dan and Matt agreed it looked something like a camel—with one hump.

Since Dan had a day off from school he decided to go fishing. That was not a very hard decision for him to make—even if he had to go by himself, as you can understand since I told you how much Dan liked to fish. He asked his mother to make him some of his favorite sandwiches: cheese on the raisin bread they used in those days. She made five of them. Dan put the five sandwiches in his basket with his bait, picked up his fishing pole, and started for the lake. But why am I saying all this? Let's let Dan tell his own story. All right, Dan.

"I'll be glad to. I could talk about that *big happening* all day long. You see, I was sitting there fishing and getting a bit tired of waiting for the fish to bite. I knew there were no big fish around because I could see a school of minnows playing around. I thought a big fish might spot them and swing in after them almost any time, but this did not happen. I had caught two small fish, but they were nothing to talk about. In fact, I kept them alive on a string so I could let them go if I caught some bigger ones.

"Then I noticed a crowd gathering over on the side of the hill, and I could hear a man talking—sort of preaching to them. I listened, but I could not hear what he was saying. More and more people were gathering, some of them running to join the crowd, so I thought I would go over there and see what it was all about. I took the two fish I had caught and put them in my basket beside my lunch. They were really too small to take home, but if I didn't bring any fish home my younger brother, Timmy, would make fun of me and say, 'I'll cut off the bottom of your robe because you didn't catch a fish.' Of course, to him a fish is a fish, even if it is a minnow.

"When I got to the edge of the crowd and could hear the man speaking, I thought I had never heard anything so interesting. The man's voice was so different. He really meant what he was saying. Just as I came up he was talking about a treasure somebody had hidden in a field. *Boy,* I thought, *I wish I could find that!* I thought he might give some hint as to where it was hidden, but then he said a man had already found it. It must have been a real prize, for the man looked up the owner of the field where he had found it and bought the whole field so there would be no question about the treasure being his. I never heard of anything like that before, but when he went on talking I saw he was showing how important it was to be a citizen of a kingdom he was telling about.

"Then, all of a sudden, I began to realize who this man was. My father had been telling us about a great prophet who was traveling in our part of the country. In fact, many thought he was the Messiah we were expecting to come. This great prophet often talked about a kingdom, and he did not mean either the Roman Empire or the Kingdom of Judah. It was something altogether different. So I listened with both ears. I wanted to learn all about that kingdom.

"To show how much people wanted to be in his kingdom, he said it was like a very valuable pearl. He said if a person saw a pearl like that he would want it so much he would sell almost all his goods to get the money to buy it.

"Now I could go on talking about that sermon because I believe I remember almost every word of it—but I must get on to the part that was really important for me. Quite a bit later, when everybody was getting hungry, I noticed that some of the men who were standing near the teacher went up and said something to him. Then these men moved through the crowd. One of them came up to me and said, 'Son, what's in your basket?' I said, 'That's just my lunch and two little fish I caught.' 'Let me see the fish,' he said. 'I am a fisherman, too.' I apologized for the tiny fish, but he said, 'Son, we all have our good days and our bad days, and sometimes we have to settle for pretty small fry.' Then he said, 'What kind of lunch did you bring?' I told him just five cheese sandwiches on raisin bread, and he asked me if he could take them to the teacher. Of course, I told him to take them along, and the fish too if he could use them.

"Then is when the *big thing* happened. When this new fisherman friend of mine took my lunch to the teacher, he held up his hand to the crowd and told them all to sit down on the ground. Then he gave a prayer and began breaking up my sandwiches. I don't know what happened, for I could not see down to where the teacher was; but the men around him began carrying out pieces of bread on palm leaves they had pulled off some nearby trees, and soon everybody was having a picnic lunch. It was great.

"The fisherman who had asked me for my lunch came back and thanked me again. I couldn't see that I had done anything important, but he said it was just what the teacher needed to help him feed that whole crowd. I told my friend to tell the teacher he could have anything I owned, any time he wanted it.

"Well, I guess that is enough about the *big happening* that day when I went fishing, but I could keep on talking about it if you wanted to listen. It was the most important day in my whole life."

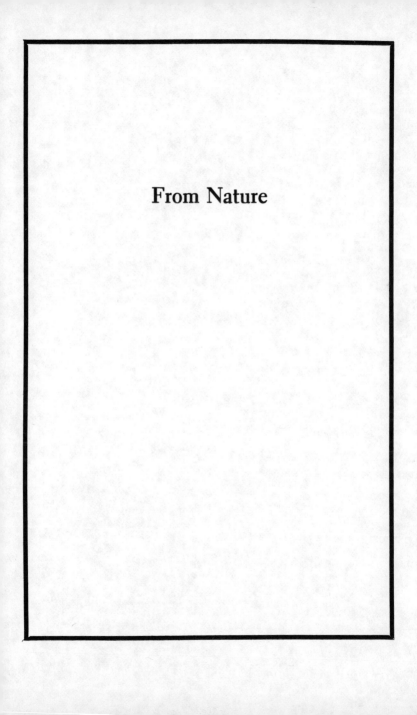

From Nature

17. Making a Pearl

And to keep me from being too elated by the abundance of revelations, a thorn was given me in the flesh, a messenger of Satan, to harass me, to keep me from being too elated (2 Cor. 12:7).

We think of diamonds, rubies, emeralds, sapphires, and other precious stones as jewels and ornaments. In earlier times these stones were worn not as ornaments but as charms to ward off evil spirits. Perhaps in some places this is still true. Most gems are of mineral formation, but pearls develop in living organisms—oysters, mussels, clams, and other freshwater and saltwater shellfish.

Off the shores of Australia, many islands of the South Seas, and the islands of Japan, divers go down to the ocean bottom to find shells that hold pearls. These are usually oysters, and the shells that have pearls inside are often the ones with the roughest texture—the ones that are oddly shaped or deformed. This is not necessarily so, but the very process that forms a pearl may cause these irregular shapes.

Pearls are caused by irritants that lodge inside the oyster shell. The object may be a grain of sand, a piece of bone or shell, or almost anything that does not belong there. Then the oyster handles the intruder by folding over it a layer of iridescent substance known as mother-of-pearl. In fact, many layers may be folded over—and the more layers the larger the resulting pearl. This mother-of-pearl is the smooth, hard surface that lines the shell.

Because shellfish react in this way to irritants, it has been found that it is possible to produce pearls artificially. Such pearls are called cultured pearls. The process is to bring up young oysters from the ocean floor, open the shells, and insert something to act as an irritant.

51

Then the oysters are put into cages to protect them from their enemies and to keep from losing them in water currents. They are then lowered again to the ocean bottom. A year later they are lifted up and examined to see how they are progressing, but it takes from five to seven years for the pearls to mature.

Pearls are divided as to size and color. Some are much more valuable than others, but all genuine pearls are of value. it takes many sizes of pearls to make a necklace graded from small to large and back to small again. Or a necklace can be made of pearls of the same size. Pearls are also used for earrings, brooches, rings, and so forth.

Because of the way pearls are formed, an analogy is sometimes made referring to people and the way they handle trouble that forms an irritant or disappointment in their lives. Most of us have troubles at one time or another, and people react differently. Some are patient and determined to find a solution to their problem and, through persistence and faith, handle it so well they win the applause of their friends. Others "fly off the handle" and become bitter and resentful and complain to the point that not only they, but also others around them, are made to feel miserable.

As we look at history—or even look around us at people we know in our community, we admire persons who have overcome handicaps so heroically that their lives shine out like living gems. Think of such a person as Helen Keller, for instance. She was blind, deaf, and dumb (could not utter a sound). Through the dedicated care of Miss Anne Sullivan, her teacher, Helen learned to read, to write, and even to speak. She received a very fine education and not only enjoyed life but made a great contribution to others. She became a world figure and traveled everywhere encouraging the handicapped. She wrote books and made speeches, and her very presence was a challenge to all who met her. Surely she made a wonderful gem of her life.

The apostle Paul had some kind of irritant in his life. We do not know what it was. He called it a "thorn in the flesh." He desperately wanted to get rid of it; but, as he says, he prayed to God, who said it was best for him to suffer with it and overcome it by patience and faith. We often wonder if the very irritant or trouble did not contribute much to his success. He said, "When I am weak, then I am strong" (2 Cor. 12:10). In his weakness he depended upon God.

52

18. Bananas

I was hungry and you gave me food (Matt. 25:35).

If we were to try to name the universal fruit—the fruit people all over the world know and enjoy eating—it would probably be the banana. People of all races eat bananas. People of all professions and all classes enjoy them. When it comes to bananas the generation gap is forgotten; fathers and mothers, grandparents, young people, children, and even babies like them. If "an apple a day keeps the doctor away," it may be said that the banana keeps nobody away but draws everybody together with its delicious taste and easy-to-eat texture.

Bananas are usually eaten raw. They are always clean and ready to enjoy. Just peel off the skin and there they are, safe and good, without washing, without cooking, without anything more to be done. Of course bananas can be cooked, and many people prefer them that way. They can be served as a salad or cooked in pies, cakes, and bread—and who doesn't enjoy a banana split! In fact, a banana is a whole meal in itself: salad, main dish, and dessert. To enjoy a good lunch all you need is a banana, a sack of peanuts, and a glass of milk. The banana is good for your health, too. In the banana you have carbohydrates and vitamins A, B, and C. No one needs to learn to like bananas; the first taste is satisfying.

We usually see only one kind of banana, the large yellow ones, but there are more than three hundred different kinds. Some are red, some yellow, some green. Some are large, some small. The people of the Philippines enjoy a small green banana, and they think it is much better than either the large red ones or the yellow ones. They usually cook this little green banana.

We often have wrong ideas about bananas. When we see large bunches hanging in the store we probably think they grow on a tree just that way, but they do not. In the first place they grow up, not down: and in the second place they do not grow on a tree. The stalk they hang from may look like a tree, but it is just a sheaf of leaves tightly wrapped around each other. There is no trunk. In the center or core is a hole, and up through this hole or channel comes the bud or blossom. After it reaches the top, probably ten or fifteen feet from the ground, it bends over and develops into the banana fruit.

Banana plants are short-lived. They bear only one crop, usually only one bunch of bananas, and then are cut down. But new sprouts immediately spring up from the roots, and soon another banana plant is growing. The process continues on and on for years. Bananas are grown on plantations with hundreds of plants in rows. These are in tropical countries, for the banana requires a hot climate. The bananas we buy in America come from Central America, Mexico, and Brazil—also the West Indies. Bananas are picked green and can be kept for weeks and even months if put in cold storage. This makes it possible to ship them great distances and still have them arrive in good condition.

The banana plant is also useful for purposes other than fruit. The broad leaves, a foot or more wide and from eight to ten feet long, can be used to thatch roofs or to weave into baskets and mats, and the fiber can be made into a coarse type of rope. Bananas are world travelers and citizens of all nations. Since everyone likes them, and since they are good, healthful food, they are helping solve one of our biggest problems: hunger.

If the banana could talk, it would speak in every language around the globe. And I think it would say, "All you people, gather around, eat my delicious food, and enjoy yourselves." Then, if we stretch our imaginations quite a bit, we might see a tremendous bench extending all around the world (a table would not be needed), and we would see smiles and happy faces and hear friendly voices talking and singing like one big family at mealtime.

19. Trees

He is like a tree planted by streams of water (Ps. 1:3).

Although we have trees growing all around us, not many people can name very many of them. In most of our cities there are oak trees, elms, sycamores, maples, pines, hemlocks, birches, poplars, and so forth. Many of these are seen along the streets and highways, and many kinds of fruit trees grow in backyards. There is one way you can tell the kind of fruit tree. If it has pears on it, it is a pear tree; if apples, an apple tree; if peaches, a peach tree—that is, if it is not grafted. By the process of grafting it is possible for many different kinds of fruit to grow on the same tree.

Did you ever see a "sucker" bush? It is just a tree branch stuck in the ground with candy suckers tied on to look like fruit hanging down. You could have a sucker bush in your backyard and invite your friends in for a party. Try it!

Fruit hanging on a tree may look attractive, but that does not necessarily mean that it is good. Sometimes you bite into a rosy apple and find a worm inside—or as someone has said, even worse, you find half a worm. Some apples are very sour, some bitter, and some knotty and not worth pulling off the tree. But not all are bad. Some apples are so beautiful and so delicious that they are carefully pulled from the tree, wrapped separately in soft paper, packed in gift boxes, and sent all over the country.

What is true of apples is also true of peaches, cherries, plums, pears, oranges, lemons, grapefruit, persimmons, and all kinds of fruit—those grown in the temperate zones and those grown in tropical climates. People everywhere enjoy fruit; and although they sometimes become tired of the fruit grown in their part of the country, they are glad to get fruit from other parts of the country. Good apples do not grow in Florida, but oranges do. People in the north enjoy oranges, and Floridians are delighted to get a box of apples from Michigan or the state of Washington.

Trees do a lot more than bear fruit. The wood of most trees is good for building houses, for furniture, for musical instruments, for ornaments, and so forth. Trees also supply the logs for our fireplaces. The bark of some trees is used for tanning hides and the resins from some for chemicals and medicines. The sap of the sugar maple is boiled down into syrup and sugar, and that is as good as candy.

The California sequoias and redwoods are the oldest, tallest, largest living things in the world. One redwood in California has a tunnel through it large enough to drive an automobile through. Another is hollowed out, and the hollow is sufficiently large to house an entire souvenir shop. A large church building in Santa Rosa, California, was built from the lumber obtained from a single redwood tree.

Redwood trees are the tallest trees in the world. In the Redwood National Park in California the trees average from 200 to 300 feet in height (the height of a thirty-story building), the tallest one being 368 feet. On these tall trees the lowest limbs are 80 to 100 feet from the ground. The oldest of these trees is a sequoia in the Sequoia National Park in California. It is called the General Sherman, and its age is estimated to be 3,500 years. If that estimate is correct, the General Sherman tree was standing in this forest at the time when the pyramids were being built in Egypt and would have been about 1,500 years old when Christ was on the earth. Amazing!

Many people think of trees as friends and feel a great loss when trees grow old and die or suffer from disease and must be cut down. Many happy memories are associated with trees—in an old orchard, at a birthplace, in a school yard, at a favorite campsite. Perhaps this is the reason that the psalmist used the tree as the symbol of a good person. In the first Psalm we read:

> He is like a tree
>   planted by streams of water,
> that yields its fruit in its season,
>   and its leaf does not wither.
> In all that he does, he prospers (Ps. 1:3).

If you think about a person as the symbol of a tree, many things might occur to you. He can grow tall and spread out his arms like tree branches to welcome and encourage others; he can make useful things and do good turns for others—which is like fruit, and he can be refreshing to all he meets—friendly, kindly, hospitable. The psalmist rightly began his poem with "Blessed is the man" (Ps. 1:1).

20. Rainbows

I set my bow in the cloud, and it shall be a sign of the covenant between me and the earth (Gen. 9:13).

Everyone has seen a rainbow arching across the sky and been delighted with its beauty. People have been looking at rainbows as far back as there have been people to look. They have wondered about them, asked questions, and tried to explain them. Greek and Roman philosophers studied them; mathematicians have added their contributions; and great astronomers have worked on the problem. Satisfactory explanations have been given, but they are rather complicated. But even if we do not understand how rainbows happen, we can enjoy their beauty.

One thing we know from observation: All the colors of the spectrum are there. From outside to inside the colors are red, orange, yellow, green, blue, indigo, and violet. Sometimes there is a second rainbow just beyond the first but not as distinct. Interestingly, the colors of this second bow are just the reverse of the main rainbow: Violet is the outside color and red the inside one.

An old folk myth says that there is a pot of gold at the end of the rainbow, but not one has ever been able to find the rainbow's end—it is too misty and indefinite. But the rainbow is a beautiful symbol of God's presence and love. There are many symbols. Shakespeare said man finds "tongues in trees, books in the running brooks, sermons in stones, and good in every thing." Many poets have voiced the fact that God can be seen in every flower, in every sunrise and sunset, in every blade of grass, and in every single thing he has created. It takes eyes to see—that is, eyes of understanding. When we look with the inner eye of faith we see more than just the appearance; we see meaning and true beauty.

The psalmist saw this beauty, and he felt the presence of God in all out-of-doors.

> The heavens are telling the glory of God;
>> and the firmament proclaims his handiwork.
> Day to day pours forth speech,
>> and night to night declares knowledge (Ps. 19:1–2).

The prophet Isaiah wrote like a poet—

> The mountains and the hills before you
>   shall break forth into singing,
> and all the trees of the field shall
>   clap their hands (Isa. 55:12).

Jesus spoke of planting seed, referred to the harvesting of the ripened grain, and likened our lives to branches on a vine, depending upon him for strength. Jesus always saw God in everything about him.

Rainbows can be seen in the mist from waterfalls (like Niagara) or even in the spray from a hose in the yard. But they usually follow a rain and sometimes even a severe storm. But what about rainbows and other beautiful things like sunsets and roses and spring flowers in the woods and the misty haze of an Indian summer morning? None of these things are really necessary. We cannot eat them or wear them, so why does God bother to make them? *Why?*

21. Squirrels

Never flag in zeal, be aglow with the Spirit, serve the Lord (Rom. 12:11).

In many of our cities, squirrels make themselves at home and supply entertainment for everyone. Cats and dogs like to chase them, and they seem to enjoy the sport. They will run and climb a tree, then move down as far as they dare and bark at their pursuer. They sometimes drop to the ground and dash for another tree just to be chased. But did you ever see a cat or dog catch a squirrel? What would he do with it if he did?

If you have squirrels in your yard or on your block, you can make friends with them. They like all kinds of nuts, especially peanuts; and their favorite tidbits are sunflower seeds. If you want to invite some squirrels to your place, put some peanuts and sunflower seeds on the window ledge and then add a sandwich or two made of bread or crackers and peanut butter. You will have fun watching them nibble away. They crack the sunflower seeds and eat them so quickly that you cannot follow the action, even if you are just on the other side of the window-pane. But if you start putting food out for squirrels and then forget to someday, look out! The squirrel that has been coming for a treat will sit up on his haunches and look in your direction with an expression that clearly says: "Say, you, why did you forget my nuts? Bah to you!" He may shake his tail at you and chatter. But the next day, when you remember to put out the seeds and nuts, he will forget bygones and be a ready guest again.

If you have a bird feeder in the yard, squirrels will try hard to get to it. You may put a baffle or some obstruction on the pole to keep them from climbing, but they will probably figure out some way to get up there. They will sit and look at the feeder, cock their heads one way and the other as though they were thinking, and may even climb a tree nearby and jump over to the feeder. It is difficult to outguess a squirrel.

Squirrels are acrobats. They are also show-offs. Sometimes they will put on a performance just for your benefit if you are watching them. See that one down there? He is turning somersaults, over and over.

Then he looks your way to see if you are looking. He will dash across the yard like a flash, dart up a tree, jump from limb to limb, swing way out on a branch, and then probably finish his act by running out of the yard on a high-strung telephone wire. He puts on a good show.

Squirrels are very curious creatures. They will go over and take a good look at every new thing they see. It may be the wrapping on a tree. They will often pull it to see what is hidden underneath. They will dig up the ground if they saw you plant something and find out for themselves what it was. Of course, they bury a lot of things. Whenever they have more of anything than they can eat they will bury the extra part, whatever it is—even bread. Then, later, they will try to find it and dig it up. When you see the many holes squirrels dig when looking for their own hidden treasures, you wonder what filing system they use to remind themselves of the hiding places. Maybe they follow the idea that if they did enough holes they may not only uncover their own hidden treasure but also discover others in the process.

Some squirrels like to collect interesting objects and store them away in a hollow tree. The caretaker of a city park near a golf course tells of finding a squirrel's hiding place in an old tree where he had stowed away about a peck of golf balls! He certainly did not mistake them for walnuts. He probably just liked to look at them or to roll them around. Who knows? If the golfers in that neighborhood had known about that squirrel's hiding place, they might have found all their lost balls.

One thing is true of all squirrels: they are very active creatures. They never seem to stop moving. They jump, dart, climb, run, twist, and jerk constantly. The apostle Paul got many illustrations for his writings by observing activities around him. When he said, "Never flag in zeal" could he have been watching a squirrel?

22. Fish

Follow me and I will make you become fishers of men (Mark 1:17).

In the city library you can find a number of books on fishing. You will notice that most of them have been read by a lot of people. Almost everyone likes to fish, and catching fish is not easy. There are many things to learn if one is to be successful. Some fishermen speak of using tricks to catch fish. Of course, the real trick is to make the bait look so natural that the fish will think it is the real thing.

Fishermen swap a lot of stories and ideas about fishing. One fisherman said, "Trout are smarter than the fishermen." The other fisherman corrected him. He said: "That trout you are trying to catch is not smart, but nature is on his side. In other words, you are not matching your wit against that of the fish. You are testing your skill against nature. A trout does not look at a bait and think, 'Is that good food or not?' He simply reacts from instinct. For instance, when a worm comes down the stream all doubled up, it may actually frighten a trout because a worm is not normally like that. It is very unnatural. If an artificial feather fly hits the water with a splash, it should cause a fish to dart away. A real insect is so light that it can land on the water daintily without making a ripple on the surface. If a fish is in a feeding mood, he is likely to take what appears normal and probably will actually avoid something that is unnatural and queer to him."

Many stories are told about expert fishermen and their tricks. Here is one: A fish was seen rising in a deep hole clear over near the far bank of the stream. How to get the bait over there in a natural way was the problem. This fisherman pulled a leaf off a nearby tree, laid his bait on the leaf, and started it floating toward the place where the fish had been rising. Then, when it was right over the exact spot, he gave his line a light twitch and caused the bait to drop into the water as if it had crawled off the leaf. The story concludes by reporting that a tremendous granddaddy trout grabbed the bait. After a long fight, the fisherman finally landed it. It weighed ten pounds!

Here's another one. A fisherman hooked a bucktail spinner (which is intended to look like a minnow swimming) just back of a feather fly. When pulled through the water, it was supposed to appear to be a small fish chasing a fly for his lunch. Fish are by nature cannibals; that is, they eat other fish smaller than themselves. There are no fish rules to prevent one fish from grabbing another fish's lunch—even including the other fish himself. So you can finish the story. The result may have been hooking a much larger fish than the one mentioned above. Can't you picture that whopper in your mind?

We like to fish and to talk about fishing because we are told that Jesus' best friends, his disciples, were fishermen. He sometimes went fishing with them. They did not use rods, reels, lines, and hooks; they fished with nets. They were commercial fishermen. They sold the fish they caught, and they needed to catch large numbers to make their work profitable. When we read the twenty-first chapter of John we learn that Jesus was a better fisherman than the men who made their living by fishing. We are told that seven of the disciples went fishing, fished all night, and caught nothing. Jesus came to them and suggested that they throw the net on the other side of the boat. This time they caught so many fish that their nets began to break.

Since Jesus' disciples were fishermen and could understand fishermen's language better than any other, he said to them, "Follow me and I will make you become fishers of men." As we read the book of Acts we learn what successful fishermen they were in the greatest business on earth—catching men and women, young people, boys, and girls for Christ and his kingdom.

Familiar Things

23. God's Workshop

God blessed them, and God said to them, "Be fruitful and multiply, and fill the earth and subdue it" (Gen. 1:28).

The first chapter of Genesis tells an amazing story. It is thrilling to read. It is an account of God's creation of the universe and the world and all living things. Of course, in such a short story a lot of details are left out; and much must be filled in by the imagination. It would seem that God purposely completed some parts of his creation and left some other parts unfinished. The unfinished parts were for his children to discover and develop. Every father enjoys working with his children and watching them discover new things, and undoubtedly this is also satisfying to God, our heavenly Father.

For instance, God completed his great laws of nature: gravity, the laws of physics and chemistry, and the basis of mathematics. Man can study these laws, learn how they work, and use them; but he cannot change them in the least. One of man's greatest physical accomplishments was using God's laws of space to go to the moon and to send the Viking spacecraft to Mars.

For use in his workshop, God left some of his wonders unfinished so that man could find them and learn how to use them. For instance: God put coal, oil, and gas deep in the ground. Man has discovered all of these and found ways to use them to heat houses, to melt and shape gold, silver, copper, and iron, and to power engines for ships, automobiles, trains, and airplanes.

God put electricity in the air everywhere for his children to find, to learn to harness, and to use to light homes and run all kinds of machinery. Man's ingenuity in using electricity makes life easier.

God put wild animals, birds, fish, and plants of all kinds all over his earth for man to tame, to train, to experiment with and develop, and to use to make life better. So man domesticated the horse, the cow, the sheep, the goat, the chicken, the pig, and a lot more. He also developed new kinds of flowers, fruits, and vegetables to grow in the fields, on his farms, and in his backyard.

You know all these things, but it is good to think about them when we see something like this beautiful American Beauty rose. Did you ever see a wild rose, often called "sweet-brier?" It is often found climbing old rail fences in the country. It is pretty, but very simple—just one row of petals. Look at this beautiful rose. You could not count the compact and lovely petals. If you could look down the years you would see that this rose came from the wild rose. Botanists for years kept experimenting with wild roses until they finally produced the American Beauty and hundreds of other roses we see in gardens today.

Here is another sample of what man has come up with in God's workshop: a big, luscious golden Delicious apple. Did you ever see a wild crab apple? Did you ever taste one? It is tiny, and it is sour! Yet this sweet Delicious apple and the tiny sour crab apple belong to the same family. Horticulturists—scientists who work with fruit trees—spent many long years developing the big sweet apple from the small sour one. They did it in God's workshop, and there are scores of different kinds of sweet apples in addition to this one.

Amazing and beautiful new products come out of God's workshop where God is working with his children to complete his unfinished creation. God has some part of this unfinished creation waiting for you to complete. With his guidance you can find what it is and then do your work of completing it. And do you know what? The most important incomplete something for each of us to finish is our own imperfect selves. Edwin Markham said, "In vain we build the world, unless the builder also grows."

24. Hammer, Saw, Chisel

Take my yoke upon you, and learn from me (Matt. 11:29).

Almost everyone uses a hammer at times, and the first thing learned is to hit the nail and not the thumb. Then, sooner or later, one must learn to use a saw. No piece of wood is exactly the right length, and no block fits perfectly; so the saw must be put into operation. Sawing is more difficult than hammering. It requires cutting in a straight line and at the proper angle.

Making presents for father and mother—like a sewing box or bookends or a bookcase—requires both sawing and hammering. If you have plans for a tree house or a house for your dog, you will get plenty of practice. Working with wood and making things is fun. When you can look at something you have made with your hands and skill, you feel good about it.

Not many amateurs use chisels, but they are important to a carpenter. He has chisels of many shapes and can use them to gouge and chip away the wood and fashion it just as he wants it. Art pieces in wood can be carved out by skillful workers. The chisel is the wood artist's special tool.

When we read the New Testament account of the early life of Jesus, we learn that he worked in the carpenter shop with Joseph. But not much is told of their type of work. In reading about carpenters of that time, we learn that they not only built houses and other buildings, but also made furniture and equipment used in harnessing animals (especially yokes for oxen). Undoubtedly, Jesus and Joseph made yokes. We can imagine that these yokes were works of art, perfectly shaped, sanded down, and polished so as not to scuff the animal's neck and to be attractive to the eye.

When Jesus was preaching he often used illustrations that must have come from his experience as a carpenter. He spoke of laying foundations, building houses, and planning ahead so that one would have enough money to complete the building. One of his favorite illustrations was the ox yoke. He said: "Take my yoke upon you, and learn from me." Jesus undoubtedly knew a lot about ox yokes by having made many of them and probably also by having fitted them around the oxen's necks. The illustration was to suggest that just as the oxen are able to draw a load easier when the weight is balanced on their shoulders with a yoke, so we can carry our problems better when we understand them and know their purpose. There is also another thought. An ox yoke has two sides, so the fact that the load is shared by two oxen makes it only half as heavy. The yoke that Jesus offers us gives us the privilege of having him share our problems as he carries the other side of the yoke; and the load is divided between us. But, best of all, we have the companionship of Jesus.

Think about this: Whenever you are working with a hammer and saw, remember that Jesus used the same tools. And you are working with your hands as he did, doing the same sort of thing. There is a quaint anonymous poem supposedly written by a carpenter. Here are a couple of the verses:

I don't know right where as His shed might ha' stood,
But often, as I've been a-planing my wood,
I've took off my hat just with thinking of He
  At the same work as me.

So I comes right away by myself with the Book,
And I turns the old pages and has a good look
For the text as I've found as tells me as He
  Were the same trade with me.

25. Needles

And you shall make a screen for the door of the tent, of blue and purple and scarlet stuff and fine twined linen, embroidered with needlework (Ex. 26:36).

The needle is the smallest and busiest tool in the workbox. Girls and women use needles the most, but men and boys use them at times. In fact, you might find needles almost anyplace if you looked hard. Rich people use them; poor people use them; young people, old people, people of all races and nations use them. Needles have been around for a long, long time. It is possible that the very first needle was a sliver of bone with a slit in one end. It was used to sew animal skins together with thin strips of rawhide or fibers from palm leaves or coarse grass.

You might say that the needle marked the beginning of civilization. When people began to wear some kind of covering for their bodies, they needed to have the pieces sewn together. The more complex the needs of people became, the more need there was for the needle and sewing. Not only was it necessary for clothing but also for tents, saddles, pouches, and for articles large and small.

As civilization advanced and as new and improved ways of living were introduced, the needle itself became altered to fit the new day. The doctor needed a hollow needle for hypodermics. He also needed a short, curved needle for sewing up wounds and incisions. The phonograph required a needle, too—one that was short and tough on the point. It was the same needle idea with a new turn to meet a new use.

The biggest problem inventors have is learning to think in new channels. For instance, when men first began trying to construct a flying machine, they tried to imitate birds and made artificial wings that would flap. They soon found this to be too complicated and cumbersome. They then turned to the idea of the kite and realized that if they could find a substitute for the kite string, to hold their craft into the wind, they might be able to rise into the air like a kite. The propeller was the answer. The earliest automobiles were called "horseless carriages." Whenever the idea of a vehicle to carry people was thought of, it was natural to think of the horse and buggy. That is why the engine was put at the front of the automobile instead of in the rear. Whoever heard of a horse at the back of a buggy? (That would be "putting the cart before the horse.")

So it was that Elias Howe's greatest problem in inventing the sewing machine was contriving a machine that would drive a needle through cloth with the eye at the rear end. The matter of wheels and gears could be solved, but how was he to get that pesky needle clear through the cloth with the eye at the rear? This may seem obvious now, but it was not in 1840. (The sewing machine was invented in 1846.) Elias worked nine years on his problem; and then he had a dream or nightmare and found his solution. He dreamed he was being chased by savages who were carrying spears with holes in the spearhead, right up at the pointed tip. There was the idea he needed: put the eye of the needle in the pointed end rather than in the rear! When he turned the needle around with the eye at the front, the rest was easy sailing.

The making of an ordinry needle may seem to be an easy matter, but it really is not. Needles must be made of very fine spring steel, which must be straightened and tempered. It takes twenty operations to manufacture a needle, and all these operations must be done with precision and skill.

The needle has worked everywhere and has met the needs of all kinds of people in thousands of ways. Through the years it has also served in the Lord's house. Careful needlework adds to the beauty and solemnity of the sanctuary. This has been recognized from early days. In the book of Exodus we read about the equipment for the tabernacle: "And you shall make a screen for the door of the tent of blue and purple and scarlet stuff and fine twined linen, embroidered with needlework" (Ex. 26:36).

That was written a long time ago, and workers carried out the request. All through the years since, dedicated fingers with needles have been serving the Lord. Close your eyes and see the busy hands today— older women with experience and skill, younger women with firm hands and nimble fingers, and girls eager to learn and to do their part, chatting, humming, singing—all having a good time because they are adding something to the beauty of the sanctuary of the Lord.

70

26. Balloons

I press on toward the goal for the prize of the upward call of God in Christ Jesus (Phil. 3:14).

Balloons! We see them at circuses, at parades, at auctions, at new car sales, at birthday parties; and Junior gets one when he takes his first trip to the barbershop. They are very familiar objects and come in all the colors of the rainbow. They have been familiar for many, many years. Balloons can be fun; they can also be put to work. They are being used regularly by weather stations all over the country to carry aloft instruments to record atmospheric conditions at different altitudes.

In earlier days when men were thinking about flying machines, the beginnings were made with balloons. It is said that two brothers named Jaques and Joseph Montgolfier made the first successful balloon. They lived in France, and their ideas that led to the construction of a balloon probably resulted from careful observation of rising smoke. They decided that a lightweight bag filled with smoke would also go up in the air. Later they found it was not the smoke but the hot air that went up, so they filled a cloth bag with hot air and got good results.

Just as in most experiments, attempts are made with animals before risking persons. And so it was in flying with balloons. History records that the first living things to fly in a balloon were a duck, a chicken, and a sheep. They were carried up quite a distance and then landed safely. This first step having been taken, it was not long until a second step was made with persons as passengers. However, the first experiments with persons were made with "captive" balloons—that is, balloons tethered to the ground with ropes or cables so they could not drift away.

It was not long before men began to vie with one another to see who could rise to the greatest height and float the greatest distance from the starting point. It seems to be always true that when one person does something unusual in any field, others must try to outdo him. Balloon contests were staged both for height and distance. As to height, the first flight recorded rose to about 500 feet. The highest record was about 114,000 feet, and the longest distance flown was about 1,900 miles. All of this was a good beginning toward the solution of the problem of flying.

From seeing the Goodyear blimp flying above us in our own hometown, we know something of the way balloons are harnessed and made to serve as flying machines. There are three kinds of gases that can be used to inflate a balloon, but only one of these is safe. Both hydrogen and coal gas are lighter than air, but both are explosive. Helium is the third gas. It has lifting power, and it will not explode. It can be safely used in a blimp. With a motor-driven propeller the blimp, carrying a gondola, can carry several persons and travel across country at a fair rate of speed.

Even the hot-air balloons are still used for exhibition purposes. To promote a carnival or other big gathering, a balloon is inflated with hot air; and a daring balloonist rises to the heights and then descends in a parachute. The balloon, relieved of the weight below, turns over, becomes deflated, and slithers down to the ground.

Some people have always wanted to fly. Perhaps the desire comes from watching birds soar so gracefully; perhaps it is natural to want to rise above the earth and see everything from a new angle. Perhaps God put the desire there. The determination to try to do better and be better every day is certainly commendable. The apostle Paul expressed it in these words: "I press on toward the goal for the prize of the upward call of God in Christ Jesus."

27. Books

Thy word is a lamp to my feet and a light to my path (Ps. 119:105).

Books have been likened to many things. For instance, it has been said that a book is like life itself—each page a day and each chapter a month. Then it would take many volumes to make a complete life. It also has been said that books take us on journeys. You can take a journey on a bus, in an automobile, on a boat, or an airplane. In imagination you can journey to another world with a good book.

Books have also been called the best of friends. One evening a group of people were being entertained by the readings of poems. The poems were well presented, and the program was very interesting. Many of the poems were written by the speaker. Great surprise arose when it was whispered through the audience that the reader was a coal miner. How in the world could a coal miner perform like that? How could a miner know anything about poetry?

Someone was bold enough to ask the question directly to the speaker. He was glad to answer. He said, "Yes, I work all day with my pick and shovel in the mine, but when the whistle blows I lay down these tools and go hom to spend the evening with my literary friends." When asked about these friends he said, "Oh, they are William Shakespeare, Sir Walter Scott, William Wordsworth, Charles Dickens. . . ." Certainly books were wonderful friends for that miner.

Books have been called mines—not of gold or silver or even of coal or iron. Books are mines of good ideas. Books are also called food and drink for the spirit. Certainly reading a good book can pick us up, inspire us, and send us on our way with a will. Books have been called gates, opening up new roads and new opportunities for us to enter. Books are mirrors; and as we read we see ourselves as we really are. Books are guides that, like compasses, point the way to go.

In all the above we are assuming one important thing: that the book in each case is a good book. Not all books are. Some are of little worth; some are a waste of money to buy and a waste of time to read. Some books are actually dangerous. They contain ideas that

73

soil the mind to think of them and suggest evil thoughts that are degrading.

Among the many good books, some are better than others. There is one book that is far above all the rest and can be called the best of all. The Bible is more than a collection of men's ideas. It is God's Word. It is truth inspired by God and was written by men in their own language, but guided by God's Spirit.

Looking back over the things we have said about books, the Bible qualifies for all of these. It is life itself (often called the book of life); it is a true friend; it is a mine of good thoughts; it is food for the soul; it is constantly opening up dates and doors of opportunity; it takes us on long journeys into realms of truth; and it is a guide to right living, being both a compass and a chart. The Bible itself says: "Thy word is a lamp to my feet and a light to my path." What a book!

28. A Seed

The kingdom of heaven is like a grain of mustard seed which a man took and sowed in his field; it is the smallest of all seeds, but when it has grown it is the greatest of shrubs (Matt. 13:31–32).

In ancient times reference was often made to the "seven wonders of the world." They were the pyramids of Egypt, the Pharos of Alexandria (an island on which a famous lighthouse stood), the hanging gardens of Babylon, the temple of Artemis at Ephesus, the statue of Zeus by Phidias, the mausoleum at Halicarnassus, and the Colossus at Rhodes. Believe it or not, I can hold in my hand, and actually conceal in the wrinkles of my palm, something more wonderful than any of these amazing structures built by man.

Without waiting for you to guess, I will tell you that the wonderful thing I hold is an apple seed. It could be any seed, an egg, or a living cell. What I wish to talk about is life in its tiniest phase, and an apple seed is a good example. Jesus spoke of the mustard seed as being the smallest of seeds and yet growing into the largest of shrubs. In our country this kind of mustard is not known. The mustard we are familiar with is just a weed and not welcomed by farmers. It springs up wild and is a menace to their crops. So we will talk about the apple seed, as apples are welcome almost everywhere and are enjoyed by almost everyone.

Look at a tiny apple seed. It is very small, brown in color; and if you cut it open or crush it you find only a mealy white substance. Take that white substance, put it in the palm of your hand, study it, and let it fire your imagination. That insignificant bit of matter is life itself. In that tiny pinch of substance is a miraculous power too great to calculate.

Keep looking at that tiny bit of white stuff. Put it under a microscope, if you wish; but even then you will need to look with creative insight stretched out to the power of infinity to do it justice. That little seed has tremendous potential. For instance, in that bit of living something is an entire apple tree: roots, branches, leaves, sap, fruit. Not only can a living apple tree come into being from that tiny seed, but that tree may live for fifty years and bear thousands of bushels of apples. From the seeds of those apples could come thousands of other apple trees. It would be impossible to begin to number the apple trees, orchards, and plantations of orchards that are right now hiding in that tiny seed. Talk about wonders—can you imagine any greater wonder than such tremendous invisible potential!

But we need not confine our thoughts to one tiny apple seed. We could look in other directions—almost any direction. Look at a robin's egg. It is small and blue. You can hide it in your hand if you are careful not to break it. Do the same thing with the robin's egg that you did with the apple seed. Think about it. This little egg has a future bird inside. It will have feathers and wings; it will be slate gray on the back and reddish brown on the breast, with some black spots on white on the throat. It will be energetic and will search for worms on the lawn, listening for them and jerking them from their hiding places. It will have a cheerful song, easily recognized by almost everyone. It will fly south each fall to warmer climates, but will be the first bird to fly north in the spring. It will be welcomed by people all over the country as the harbinger of warm days soon to come. But this is not all. This one bird is just the beginning of a flock of robins so numerous that no one could count them—at least in that egg! In imagination we can see robin after robin, year after year, building a nest, having young, flying south, returning in the spring, building another nest, and so on and on.

When Jesus spoke of the tiny mustard seed and its amazing power, he was illustrating the power of the gospel idea. When a person who has caught the spirit of Christ is really concerned, he will share his enthusiasm with someone else, in fact with many persons—his friends, his schoolmates, people he meets from day to day. Then many of those who hear will tell the story to others; and so the gospel truth goes on and on endlessly. Apple seeds and eggs are interesting to think about; but the miracle of the gospel, acting like seed, changing lives, building a better world, is not only wonderful but is God's greatest wonder on earth.

29. Baseball

Every athlete exercises self-control in all things (1 Cor. 9:25).

Let us run with perseverance the race that is set before us (Heb. 12:1).

Baseball is called the national sport of the United States. Considering the attendance of fans at games throughout the season all over the country, it no doubt is. In addition to the professional teams, there are grade school teams, high school teams, college teams, Boy Scout teams, Little League teams, varsity teams, scrub teams, sandlot teams, Sunday School teams, pickup teams—in fact, most people in the country understand the game; and almost everyone, at some time or other, gets into the act.

Generally people are fairly well informed about the game of baseball. In almost any group of people you will find some who are able to tell you the names of all the famous players down through the years. There are plenty of fans who can tell you the difference between a curveball and a fastball, a slider and a change of pace, a screwball and a knuckle ball; and some of them can demonstrate by making some very fancy pitches.

Many people visit the Baseball Hall of Fame during their vacation travels. It is located at Cooperstown, New York. The first players selected and honored by being listed there were Ty Cobb, Babe Ruth, Hans Wagner, Walter Johnson, Christy Mathewson, and Bob Feller. Every year the best players are selected and added to the list. Cooperstown, New York, is the very place where the first diamond was laid out with the four bases sixty feet apart. The game was started in the year 1839. The Baseball Hall of Fame with its baseball museum was opened just one hundred years later, in 1939.

Every position is important in the game of baseball. We think of the "batteries" of the two teams as the pitcher and the catcher, but first base is certainly important; and so is shortstop. In fact, every base and every spot in the outfield is important. When a ball is hit, it may go in any direction and for any distance. Every player is a possible key person to catch it or make a play.

The plays are all interesting, too, in different ways. Runs are exciting whether they are one-baggers, two-baggers, or more. Home runs bring the fans to their feet, yelling, clapping, and whistling. Stolen bases are thrilling. In fact, every play is fun except when the teams are not well matched and one team piles up a big score. It is no fun either when all the bases are loaded and the team is unable to get even one runner home. But a "grand slam!" Boy! That is something!

It would seem that from the earliest times people have been interested in some kind of athletics. As you read sections of Paul's writings you find he must have watched a lot of sports events. There was no baseball, football, or basketball in Paul's day; but there were foot races—both short runs and marathons—archery both for accuracy and distance, javelin throwing, discus hurling, and a number of other tests of strength. Paul found sports very useful for sermon illustrations. Listen to these words: "Every athlete exercises self-control in all things" (1 Cor. 9:25). He also said: "Do you not know that in a race all the runners compete, but only one receives the prize? So run that you may obtain it" (1 Cor. 9:24).

The writer to the Hebrews was also a sports enthusiast, as we gather from Hebrews 12:1. "Therefore, since we are surrounded by so great a cloud of witnesses, let us also lay aside every weight, and sin which clings so closely, and let us run with perseverance the race that is set before us."

It would seem that both of these writers were stressing three traits that are illustrated by athletes: keeping in shape by practice and training, giving one's best efforts to win, and never giving up until the very end of the game. These traits are demonstrated in almost every game we see or play. Athletes must keep in training to be able to play at full strength; they must be determined to win if possible; and they must not stop until the last whistle blows. How many times we have seen a game won in the last few seconds! Isn't it fine that athletics are included in God's plan for us and that playing games with fair sportsmanship is part of the action of good living?

Attitudes

30. Who Are You?

You are the salt of the earth . . . You are the light of the world (Matt. 5:13–14).

If someone asks who you are, you may say, "I am Billy, or Susan, or Jimmy, or Mary." But really, who are you? One of the first things you learned to say when you began to talk was "Ma-ma" and "Da-da." You also soon could say "me," and that was important.

You are a person—different from your father and your mother, your brothers and your sisters. You are very special. You are *you.* For instance, you not only have a body that is different from other bodies, but you have a mind; and you think thoughts that are different from what others think. You have a will, and you decide to do this instead of that and make up your mind just what you want and what you do not want.

You are important—and right here comes a question: important to whom? A big decision must be made here. You could say, "I am important to myself, and I will do all I can to help myself to whatever looks good to me." We would have to call that just plain selfishness. A person who talked and acted like that would not be very helpful either to himself or to anyone else. He would be a "stick in the mud."

You see, you are not the only one around. There are other persons here too—lots of them, and all of them are important. In fact, your importance and their importance tie together. You and I are important because we are important to each other, and all of us are important because of what God wants us to do in the world.

For instance, you are important to your parents, and they are important to you. How would you get along without them to give you a home, food, clothes, and, most of all, love? They feel the same way about you. They certainly would not want to get along a single day without you. You are very dear to them.

You have friends. You go to school. You have a teacher (or several of them). You go to Sunday School. You are important to all these people, and they are important to you. Together you make the school and the Sunday School. Without you and your friends there would be no school or Sunday School at all.

Most of all, you are important to God. He made you and loves you. He has a very important work for you to do. I do not know what it is, and you do not yet. But in time you will, and you must be getting ready to tackle it when the right time comes. Of course, you don't have to wait until you grow up. There is plenty for you to do right now. Remember what Jesus said to his disciples: "You are the salt of the earth . . . You are the light of the world."

Those are pretty big words: salt, light. They may seem little as you think of a saltshaker on the table or a candle on a stand or an electric light on the table. Jesus was not speaking of such things. He was using these as illustrations or stepping-stones for your mind to walk up to a great idea. As salt makes food tasty and good to eat, so good people "salt" the neighborhood and make it a better place in which to live. As a candle or an electric bulb lights up the room, so boys and girls, men and women who do God's will brighten their surroundings and help others to see their way in the dark. Light stands for knowledge, understanding, and truth; and these are things all of us need a lot of.

So let's get back to our first question: Who are you? You have a name, but you are more than a name. You are *you*, and that *you* is a child of your parents who love you, a pupil of the school and the Sunday School, a friend of your friends. And, most important of all, you are a child of God. He loves you more than you could possibly weigh, measure, or count; and he has a big reason for your being here. You are to be salt for him and his light to share with others all around you and help them to know who they are, too. Yes, you are pretty important, and you have a big job to do!

31. What Are the Rules?

Any other commandments are summed up in this sentence, "You shall love your neighbor as yourself." Love does no wrong to a neighbor; therefore love is the fulfilling of the law (Rom. 13:9–10).

Every game we play has rules to guide the players. Some games have very complicated rules; some are simple. We like to make the rules as few as possible. Life itself is often called a game, and the rules are many. Through the years people have tried to define right living in simple terms. Long ago a philosopher, Immanuel Kant, said that good living could be defined as keeping two rules: (1) Treat everyone as an end and not as a means. That is, treat everyone as a person, and never try to use another for your own purpose. (2) So act that the law of your life might well become the law for all mankind. In othe words, try, in all you do, to act in such a way that it would be fine if all people everywhere copied your example.

These two rules are splendid. If everyone lived by them we would have a beautiful world. Such living would rule out all selfishness, all meanness, all violence, all thoughtlessness.

In the New Testament we find the rules for living reduced to just one big word that is alive with meaning. Paul listed all the Ten Commandments and added: "All are summed up in this sentence, 'You shall love your neighbor as yourself.' Love does no wrong to a neighbor; therefore love is the fulfilling of the law."

The big word is *love*. Love is the important word all through the New Testament. We are told that God himself can be defined in one word—written large. God is *love*. Of course, that word is not a simple one; and it is not easy to understand. Like a diamond with many facets or faces, it can be expressed in just about everything we do.

It might be illustrated by a couple of stories. The first is from the Old Testament, and the second from the New. You remember the story of Joseph, the favorite son of his father, who was given the coat of many colors. He was the boy who got into trouble with his eleven brothers because they thought their father treated him so much better than he treated them. These jealous brothers sold Joseph as a slave to traveling merchants, who sold him to Potiphar, the captain of Pharaoh's guard in Egypt.

You could tell the story yourselves, but the important part to remember is about Joseph's meeting with those brothers later. Joseph had become a powerful person in Egypt. Pharaoh had placed him in charge of his great stores of grain. When his brothers came to buy grain for their families he recognized them, but they did not realize who he was. What a chance for Joseph to get even with them! He could have had them put in prison; he could have had them beaten or killed. But he forgave them. He acted in love. What a wonderful ending to that story of jealous brothers!

The other story is one Jesus himself told. It is called the story of the prodigal son. When that son returned home after wasting his father's money and acting so badly that no one would have anything to do with him, his father ran to meet him, forgave him, and showered his love on him. Again, a great story shows what love can do with people. There is nothing like it!

The fine part about both of these stories is that they deal with something that is still the finest thing in the world. It is both old and new. It works with all kinds of people, all races, in all places, everywhere. And you and I can have it and practice it right now and every day of our lives!

32. Temptation

Lead us not into temptation, But deliver us from evil (Matt. 6:13).

Growing up is more than getting bigger and stronger. It is learning to know more, to understand better, and to live as we should. In this learning process sometimes simple everyday things are the most difficult to explain. For instance, take two sentences from the Lord's Prayer which we say so often: "Lead us not into temptation. But deliver us from evil."

We all know something about temptation, but does God ever lead us into trouble? Do we need to ask God not to cause us to be tempted? What does being tempted mean? It may have two different meanings: luring a person to do something wrong, or testing a person to see how strong he is.

This sentence in the Lord's Prayer has puzzled people through the years. I think it applies particularly to young people and to boys and girls. You are frequently daring each other to do things, usually that are dangerous or difficult. This sentence says not to take any dares to do wrong. Stay as far away as you possibly can. So the two sentences belong together: "Lead us not into temptation. But deliver us from evil." Jesus also said: "You have heard that it was said to men of old, 'You shall not kill' . . . But I say to you that every one who is angry with his brother shall be liable to judgment" (Matt. 5:21–22). In other words, we are to go as far away from evil as possible—in the opposite direction.

Let us take a couple of illustrations. Here is a girl. We will call her Alice. She likes pretty clothes and wants a dress she saw in the store window. Her mother says, "If you want it you must buy it with your allowance money." Alice does not have enough saved. She knows if she begs her aunt, her aunt will no doubt let her have the money. She also knows that would not be the right thing to do. In time she will have enough allowance money to buy the dress; but she wants it now. Alice might well pray that part of the Lord's prayer: "Lord, lead me not into temptation; deliver me from evil."

Take another illustration. Here is a boy named Russell. He has quite a temper. When things do not go the way he likes, he simply "blows up." He knows that it is wrong to give way to his temper, and he also knows that certain situations always put the pressure on him. Russell might well pray that part of the prayer: "Lord lead me not into temptation; deliver me from evil." His prayer is to be kept far away from situations that cause him to explode. If he were conceited he might brag, "Bring on the temptation—no matter how big it is, I can handle it." But he knows his weakness, and he really wants to control that temper. So he prays that the kind of encounter that causes him to flare up will be avoided. That is not cowardice, but just good sense.

If we are to develop strong characters we need to be tested. If there were only one way we could go and no decision needed to be made, we would be robots doing what we were commanded to do. We would be puppets, not persons. However, it is very foolish to go out of our way to tackle trouble to prove how strong we are. There are plenty of temptations and tests that come along which we cannot avoid. It is a very wise person indeed who prays God to make these as few as possible and asks for his presence to protect us from being overcome by the evil. "Lead us not into temptation. But deliver us from evil."

33. A Dull Day

This is the day which the Lord has made; let us rejoice and be glad in it (Ps. 118:24).

It was one of those days: dull, monotonous, dead! There was just nothing interesting to do. There were games to play, but there was no one to play them with. There were books to read, but reading didn't sound exciting at all. There were TV shows, but all of them were reruns. It wasn't raining outdoors, but it was just a gloomy, gray day. Dave took his problem to his grandmother. He was staying at her house while his father and mother were on a trip to Detroit.

Grandmother turned her head to one side, then the other. She snapped her fingers and said: "I have it! We have windows on all four sides of our house. Look out each window—look sharp—and write down everything you see that moves. We'll just find out how alive this day is even if it does seem dull and dead." That appealed to Dave. Grandmother gave him a pad of paper and a pencil, and he started with the front window.

Before he could get to the window he heard a siren. He reached the window just in time to see the flashing lights of a fire truck as it raced by. Right behind the truck came some boys running and several others on bicycles, going to the fire. Luckily, it was not a serious blaze and was soon handled by a couple of firemen with extinguishers. While Dave was watching, some tiny tots went by on their tricycles, also going in the direction of the fire truck. Another sound called attention to a jet plane zooming into the sky from the airport nearby; then a helicopter began circling overhead. It was connected with the police and fire departments and stood ready to direct activities from its advantage in the air when needed.

Dave was so interested in movements outside the front window that Grandmother had to remind him that there were other windows and other activities. So he strolled over to the kitchen window. "Grandmother, come here quick!" he called. "There's a rabbit in the backyard. I didn't know there were rabbits around here!" Grandmother explained that it was unusual for a rabbit to be in the middle of the city, but

87

this one had been hopping around the yard for about a week. She had put out an apple and some carrots for him. Then, while Dave was watching the rabbit, two squirrels started chasing each other around the yard. They must have been playing tag as they darted about, ran up a tree, ran back down, ran up another tree, ran out on a branch, and finally raced away on a telephone cable.

But back in the yard there was more action. A bluejay swooped down and snatched a peanut that had been thrown out for the squirrels; and as Dave watched, he stashed it away in a pine tree and flew back for another. In the meantime a half-dozen starlings and sparrows and a couple of grackles were greedily pecking away at some pieces of bread on the lawn. A cardinal was perched on a wire watching them.

But there were two other windows, and Dave reluctantly went to the window in the breakfast nook. As he approached the window he saw something creeping along the ground. When he reached the window ledge, he saw it was a large black and white cat sneaking up on a robin that was industriously pulling a worm out of the ground. Dave ran to the door to warn the robin and got there none too soon. Just as he opened the door the cat made a dash for the robin, which luckily took to the air just in time to escape. The cat jumped over the fence and disappeared, but Dave's attention was attracted to a large flock of pigeons circling around overhead. Soon they lighted on the roof of a neighbor's house down the street. They seemed to feel at home there and probably spent a lot of time on that roof. Down in the neighbor's yard something else was moving—a dog. Yes, a small boy was throwing a stick for the dog to retrieve; and both boy and dog seemed to be having a good time. After writing down these "moving objects," Dave moved to the last window—in the bedroom.

Believe it or not, he saw a mouse actually running up the side of the neighbor's house. Yes, a little gray field mouse with a long tail! He ran up near the corner and darted into a crack in the brick wall near the roof. The neighbor, Mrs. Godfrey, was in the yard clipping her rosebushes; and Dave wondered if he should tell her about the mouse. But even if he did, she would hardly believe that a mouse could run straight up a brick wall. But he had seen it happen. As he watched to see if the mouse would come out of the crack, he saw a pheasant fly into a thick bush at the back of the neighbor's yard. He watched for several minutes and saw the pheasant moving around on a branch, but it soon settled down and appeared to have decided that was a good place to stay.

Well, it did not take that "dull" day long to slip by. Before Dave had completed his list of things moving out the windows, his mother and father were at the door to pick him up and take him home. Yes, dull days can really be very interesting, and even exciting— sometimes.

34. Every Day

Every day I will bless thee, and praise thy name for ever and ever (Ps. 145:2).

Did you ever see a great cathedral? Have you visited our national Capitol in Washington? Have you seen the Empire State Building in New York City? When looking at a large building, do you ever wonder how long it took to construct it? In imagination you might see the workmen—steam shovel operators, stonemasons, steel construction men, carpenters, bricklayers, plumbers, electricians, glass workers—busy on the job every day, week after week, month after month until the building rose from the foundation to the completed roof.

That phrase "every day" accounts for a lot of accomplishment in countless areas. You hear a great pianist give a lovely concert. Back of that perfect technique were countless everyday hours of practice. The same is true in every line of good performance. That football team, that baseball team, that basketball team—if they are working together as a good team should and if they are playing the game in a masterful way, they show the result of practice every day, day after day, week after week.

When any person does something unusually well, be it saying a speech, acting in a play, carving a piece of wood, growing beautiful flowers, or painting a picture that "looks as real as life"—you can count on it, that person spent long hours and worked hard every day for months and years learning how to do that thing and do it well.

How does a person become good in a foreign language? You sometimes meet a person who can speak several languages as naturally as if he had lived in those foreign countries. It is the very same story: He worked at the mastery of the language hour after hour, every day for years.

Nature itself is built on that principle. The sun comes up every morning and seems to go behind the horizon every evening. The seasons come and go routinely, day by day, week by week, month by month, year by year. Looking closer, your own body operates the same way: hour by hour, day by day, your heart continues to beat and you continue to breathe; and you eat your meals regularly, every day.

Just to sit back and look at it the whole thing seems very monotonous, but that is the way it is; and the only way to get ahead in any line of endeavor is to work at it steadily every day.

Most important of all is the building of character and the good life. It is not a matter of one or two great heroic acts. It is the regular, consistent living every day that counts and produces the personality that people admire and that serves usefully in the community. The Bible emphasizes the importance of everyday performance. The psalmist said, "Every day I will bless thee, and praise thy name for ever and ever."

It is amazing what can be accomplished working on that everyday principle. Things that seem impossible and that would be out of the question if one attempted to complete them all at once can be handled if tackled one day at a time. Jesus once spoke about the problems people have. They are many and varied. Some are very serious and others not so bad, but all seem big and important at the time they are faced. Jesus gave a perfect rule of action: He said to deal with them one day at a time. When you come to think about it, that makes everything look different. A big job is cut down to size. One day's section of it is not bad at all. Jesus said it this way: "Do not be anxious about tomorrow, for tomorrow will be anxious for itself. Let the day's own trouble be sufficient for the day" (Matt. 6:34).

35. Go On!

When he has laid a foundation, and is not able to finish, all who see it begin to mock him, saying, "This man began to build, and was not able to finish" (Luke 14:29-30).

A stranger visiting a certain southern town was surprised to see an ugly vacant lot, grown up with weeds, right in the middle of the downtown district. When he inquired about it, he heard this story: A few years back, a preacher without a congregation, wishing to build a church house and start a worship program, solicited money for his project. As soon as he got a little cash he bought a lot and a load of stones. He had the basement dug and laid a foundation. This took all the money he had collected; and since no more money was received, he gave up his idea and left town.

Undoubtedly the city council would not allow such an eyesore to remain, and soon someone with long-range plans and enough money and determination to build something worthwhile corrected the situation.

Jesus told a story like that. The building he spoke about was not a church, but a tower; and the would-be builder was laughed at by the townspeople because he started something he could not finish. Many good ideas are allowed to die because the person who has them does not go on. He may lose his enthusiasm or lack the drive and determination to get down and work at the job. You often hear the expression: "Yes, I started that several years ago, and I expect to finish it some day."

We like to hear stories of persons who go on until they get the job done. The other day the newspaper had a story of a boy like that. His class at school was studying about government and business and citizenship—a lot of subjects that seemed too big for a grade school group to handle, but at least they could talk about them and learn something about what goes on back of the scenes in the community and in the country.

The teacher said one of the biggest problems in the country today—and in the community—was unemployment. That was a difficult word to understand. But it was easy when the teacher explained it meant people without jobs and without a chance to work and make money so their families could buy food and clothes and pay for electricity and gas and all the things they needed to live day after day. The children knew many people who did not have a job and needed one very much. In fact, several in the class had fathers who were out of work, and they knew what that meant in their own homes.

The teacher said that the children could do something about this problem. She gave the class an assignment: each child was to write a theme on the subject of unemployment and make a suggestion how to solve it. That really was a difficult job to tackle.

One boy looked at that assignment and said: "That is too big for me; I can't do a thing about unemployment." When he went home that evening he told his father and mother and said: "I just won't go to school tomorrow because I can't write that paper."

His parents told him that he must go to school and write something. They insisted that he think hard and do the best he could. They said, "Go on, you can do as well as the other boys and girls in your class."

Do you know what happened? Jim thought real hard, and he decided to write a letter. He wrote to the congressman from his town, and his letter sounded something like this:

"Dear Honorable Congressman:

Our class is studying about unemployment. It is too big for us to understand, but I have this idea to suggest: Will you please get a job for just one man who needs one? That won't do much, but it will get something started. Thank you,

Jim."

Now this may seem like a fairy tale, but Jim's letter did get something started. A man in Jim's town was given a job in a warehouse a few days later, and the congressman told him it was because of Jim's letter. This man wrote Jim and thanked him and said: "I don't know you and I don't know how you did it, but I was told by my congressman that it was in answer to your letter that he found me a job. Thank you, for I have been out of work for nearly a year and I certainly needed this job so I could pay my bills."

The same day the above newspaper story appeared there was another—with a picture of the boy it was written about. He had no arms and hands. The reason the story came out was because he was the best goal kicker in teams of his age group. As a very small boy he was told by his parents: "You can do what you want to do if you work hard enough." They would not talk about his handicap, but only about what he could do if he tried. They always told him: "Go on, you can do it." He could not catch a football, but he could kick one. He decided to keep practicing until he could kick it straighter and farther than anyone else in his class. That is exactly what he was able to do. Because of his accurate kicking, his team was a winner. He was the most valuable player in the group. They are certainly glad that long ago he determined to go on. That is still his motto: "Go on!"

36. Humbug!

Beware of false prophets, who come to you in sheep's clothing but inwardly are ravenous wolves (Matt. 7:15).

Do you know what a hypocrite is? Do you know what a humbug is? What about a "snake in the grass"? Jesus used another expression. He said some wicked people were like wolves with the skins of sheep on their backs. All of these words and expressions describe a deceiver, a person who tries to make believe he is something which he really is not.

Usually, the expression means a bad person trying to make-believe he is good or a thief trying to act like an honest person. Even animals sometimes act this way. You may have a cat that purrs and rubs against you as if he would not harm anything, but all the time there is a bird's feather hanging out of the corner of his mouth!

A hypocrite can also be a person who tries to make you believe he is worse than he actually is. There is that boy, a newcomer, who appears on the playground and wants to make the other fellows think he is a tough guy. He talks big, tells tall tales, and claims that he chews, smokes, and drinks. When you come to know him better, you may find he is telling the truth about his habits, but the truth is not what he tried to make you believe. Yes, he chews bubble gum, smokes candy cigarettes, and drinks ginger ale and root beer.

Another kind of hypocrite is someone who claims to be better than he or she is. Do you know a girl like that? To hear her talk, you would believe she has a nicer house than anyone in the crowd. She has more toys than she can handle, and they are very expensive. She herself can do everything better than anyone else around. She is such a prima donna that she will not even play with others in the block because they are not good enough for her. Of course the regrettable thing about such a person is that she is heading for a fall.

Since we know boys and girls like the ones just mentioned, the question is, how should we treat them? Both of them are misfits in the crowd that gathers on the playground. The natural thing might be to make fun of them or to just ignore them altogether. But that would not solve the problem. They both belong in the group and you should try to let them know you want them in and help them become good playmates.

We talk about being Christians in our everyday lives. We know it is easy to be Christians at church and at Sunday School, but it becomes more difficult when we get back home, when we go to school, and when we are on the ball diamond. The very kinds of persons we are talking about present a "dare" to the rest of the crowd. This is a dare to prove you know how to be a Christian outside of the church and to help others in your own group who need help. Why not decide, "We will help those two to become good sports. We can do it, and we will!"

And you can. The first move is to be good sports yourselves—toward them. The second thing is to invite them to join in your games and fun. The third thing is to treat them just like the rest of the gang when they come. You will be surprised at what will happen. Perhaps both of them are just waiting for such an invitation. It may be that their actions were just a cover-up for their loneliness or timidity. Anyway, it won't hurt to try. It might work! And if it does, you will really feel good about it!

37. Who's Afraid?

The Lord is my light and my salvation; whom shall I fear? The Lord is the stronghold of my life; of whom shall I be afraid? (Ps. 27:1).

Sometimes you hear a boy or a girl say, "I am afraid." At once you want to ask: "Afraid of what?"

Of course, there are a lot of things all of us should be afraid of: a contagious disease, playing with fire, telling a lie, or doing something we know is wrong. But if a person says, "I am afraid of the dark" or is afraid to try something just because it is new and different, then we wonder.

Almost everyone is afraid of something or afraid sometimes. For instance, a girl may be afraid of being laughed at because she does not have nice clothes like other girls. Her parents are poor and unable to buy clothes for her. A boy may be afraid to go to the playground because he cannot play ball as well as the other boys. He never had the chance to learn to throw a ball.

These are what we might call natural fears, and they can be taken care of. The girl who is afraid of being laughed at will soon find out that clothes are not all-important. The other girls will be glad to get to know her. Soon they will be talking together, playing games, and making friends, and what she thought was a problem is no problem at all.

The boy who is afraid of the playground gang because he cannot throw a ball will find that he can do some things the other boys cannot do. There was such a boy. His father did a program of tricks and juggling to entertain his friends. This boy had watched his father perform and had learned to do most of the tricks. He could juggle four golf balls at a time. You know what? The other boys heard about this, and they asked him to put on a show for them. Although he could not play baseball, he got the attention of the whole gang as they watched him do some mystifying tricks and then juggle the golf balls. In fact, he broke up the ball game for a week. All the boys wanted to learn to do the tricks, and all of them were practicing juggling!

The word afraid is used many times in the Bible because being afraid is a common experience. The psalmist gave the sure cure for all fear when he said: "The Lord is my light and my salvation; whom shall I fear? The Lord is the stronghold of my life; of whom shall I be afraid?"

The shepherds were afraid when the angel appeared to them announcing the birth of Jesus; but the angel said: "Fear not; for behold, I bring you good tidings" (Luke 2:10, KJV).

The disciples were terribly afraid when they were in the boat and the storm came up. Jesus quieted the storm (also the fear in their hearts) and said: "Why are you afraid? Have you no faith?" (Mark 5:40). Can you really understand why those disciples were afraid when Jesus was right there with them?

After the crucifixion of Jesus, when the two Marys went to the tomb on Easter Sunday morning, they were nervous and afraid. But the angel said to them: "Do not be afraid; for I know that you seek Jesus who was crucified. He is not here; for he has risen, as he said. Come, see the place where he lay. Then go quickly and tell his disciples that he has risen from the dead, and behold, he is going before you to Galilee; there you will see him" (Matt. 28:5–7).

All through the Bible we are told not to fear but to have faith. Two expressions of Jesus we might well remember. He used them often. One was, "Be not afraid." The other was, "Be of good cheer." The two really belong together; for when we are not afraid to venture out, meet others, try new things, be ourselves, and do our best, we are truly cheerful and also happy.

38. Tiptoeing

As the people were in expectation, and all men questioned in their hearts concerning John, whether perhaps he were the Christ (Luke 3:15).

The way people use their feet often indicates how they are thinking. For instance, you may see a fellow jogging by your house early in the morning. He is either training for a track event or is concerned about his health and is taking exercise. Watch that man stomping his feet, and you know there is something he does not like one bit! He is expressing his dislike by crushing it under his feet—even if it is just an idea he objects to. Then watch the person who holds his head high and leans back when he walks. He is strutting like the drum major leading the varsity band on the football field. He must be thinking pretty well of himself. Here comes a little girl hopping, skipping, jumping along. She is evidently very happy about something and is eager to get where she is going. That man with head down, shuffling his feet, just trudging along as though he were carrying a heavy burden on his shoulders, really is doing just that. He is worrying about something, and it is weighing him down. He is despondent, discouraged, downhearted. Then there is the person who walks "flatfooted." He is "down in the dumps," uninterested, just plain disgusted with everything and everybody.

But there is another way to use one's feet. That is *tiptoeing:* standing on tiptoe and looking with eyes wide open and spirits on edge. That is a wonderful way to use the feet, the toes, the mind, and the heart: to be alert and eager, to look forward to see and greet the very best that life has to offer. There are certain things one can see only when on tiptoe—for instance, the blue eggs in a robin's nest, the Fourth of July parade going by when the street is crowded with people, and a brand-new idea that is sure to bring happiness if we will recognize it and put it to use.

All the really important things that ever happen must be welcomed by people who are on tiptoe, looking forward, and expecting something good to come along. The joggers are thinking too much about themselves to notice; the stompers do not believe anything good can happen;

the strutters have their noses so high in the air they cannot see anything in front of them; the trudgers have personal burdens so heavy they cannot see or think about anything else, and the flatfooters are too dull to recognize anything but boredom.

Luke said that at the time Jesus came to earth, people in Palestine were looking for a great Messiah or leader to come. As he said, they were in "expectation." They were ready, tiptoeing, looking, hoping, and eager to greet the man from God when he appeared. Of course, not all the people were like that; but it takes at least a select group of people on tiptoe to make good things come to pass. We might use other terms for them. They are people with high hopes and great faith. They are looking forward, believing, yearning, waiting restlessly.

Jesus recognized these people. When they were around him great events took place; miracles happened. When they were absent it was difficult for him to do "any great work." We are told that when Jesus was in Nazareth, he preached in the synagogue. This was the town where he had lived as a boy, and people knew him well. They thought of him as the carpenter and the young man who had grown up there. They did not expect anything important from him since he was a hometown boy. Because of their lack of faith and their deadpan attitude, Jesus "could do no mighty work there" (Mark 6:5), and he marveled because of their unbelief.

But look what happened in another place where Jesus found a centurion who had such great faith that he caused Jesus to marvel and say: "I tell you, not even in Israel have I found such faith" (Luke 7:9). The centurion was concerned about his servant, who was paralyzed. He believed that Jesus could heal him, and Jesus was ready to go to the house, but the centurion said that was not necessary. He believed that Jesus could perform this miracle by just saying the word. This is why Jesus marveled at his faith, and he rewarded the centurion by healing his servant. In imagination we wonder what amazing things Jesus might have done in Nazareth if the people had believed and if they had been on tiptoe, expecting great things to happen.

39. Happiness Is—

Blessed are the merciful (Matt. 5:7).

Henry was really "off the track." When he came downstairs and his mother said, "Good morning, Henry," he only grunted. When she asked him what he would like for breakfast, he replied: "I don't want oatmeal and I don't want cornflakes; I'm tired of that stuff. I guess I just don't want anything; I'm not hungry."

But he did eat some French toast. His mother always tried to make the children happy, and she prepared them what they liked if she had it on the pantry shelves. So Henry was starting his day off pretty badly. He was unhappy. Anybody could see that. He must have gotten out on the wrong side of the bed. It was Saturday and he did not have school, so he could have been thinking of doing something he very much wanted to do; but that was not Henry this Saturday. He went out the door and shut it with a bang.

He started down the street without anything in mind or any place to be going. He just felt out of sorts and really did not know why. He met Mr. La Rue, who was a neighbor—a very kind one—and Henry usually chatted with him, but not this morning. He just said "Hello" and did not even add, "It's a fine sunshiny morning, Mr. La Rue." Of course, Mr. La Rue knew that. But it is nice to express our appreciation for a bright morning, and there isn't much to say to a neighbor you see every day. But Henry didn't act very friendly. Perhaps Mr. La Rue did not think anything of it, for he was always thinking the best of everyone.

A fellow schoolmate rode by on his bike and called out to Henry, "See you on the ball diamond this afternoon, Henry." Henry just said, "Yah, I guess so," but he did not say it with much enthusiasm. He just went on down the street with his head down as though the whole world were against him when, actually, he was the one out of step.

Down at the corner of Ottawa and Butler he saw a small boy sitting on the curb crying. Just then a car went by so close to the child that Henry rushed to the youngster and lifted him onto the sidewalk. He asked the boy his name. "My name is Johnny," he said. "Where

101

do you live?" asked Henry. The boy could not tell him; neither could he tell him his last name. He just kept saying, "I want Mommy; I want Mommy."

Henry did not know what to do, but he was sure his mother would know; so he coaxed the youngster to walk along with him toward his home. He was a tiny one and could not walk very fast, but he was willing to toddle along. So they moved very slowly toward Henry's home. Henry tried to talk with the youngster, but he did not get very far. He was not interested in conversation. All he wanted was his mommy.

When Henry reached his home it was a rather humorous sight to see Henry trying to get the little fellow to go into the house with him. He did not want to go into a strange house. But Henry's mother heard the commotion out in the yard and came to the rescue. She knew how to handle youngsters; and although she was not his mommy, she acted just like his mommy. The child was comforted.

Henry and his mother talked the matter over. They had never found a lost child before, but they had read about such cases. Usually the parents would inquire at the police station to find if anyone had seen the lost youngster. So Henry decided to call the police station. Sure enough, a mother was there at the station looking for her lost boy. She gave a description of the little fellow Henry had brought to his home, and Henry could hear her happiness over the phone to know that her little boy was safe. She asked for the number of Henry's house and said she would be over immediately.

You can imagine the joy of that mother when she picked up Johnny at Henry's home and the joy of the little boy who had found his mommy—and, would you believe it, the joy of Henry because he had made someone else happy. Yes, that very day Henry learned what happiness is.

Special Days

40. Freedom Is—
INDEPENDENCE DAY

For you were called to freedom, brethren; only do not use your freedom as an opportunity for the flesh, but through love be servants of one another (Gal. 5:13).

Carl and Alice were agreed on one thing: They wanted to enjoy a week of "absolute freedom." School had been long; both of them had worked hard and finished the year with good grades. Now, for at least one whole week, they wanted to be as free as the wind. What would be freer than a week in the wilderness, living in a tent, sleeping in the out-of-doors, and doing just what you wanted to do? Carl liked fishing. He never could get enough of it. Alice was crazy about wild flowers. She was making a collection of rare and beautiful ones, pressing them, and mounting them in a book.

Mother listened in on their conversation about freedom, and she made them a proposition. They could use the family tent; she would ask Dad to transport it wherever they wanted to go—within reason— and each of them would accept and faithfully do their chores. So they had a huddle and decided that Carl was to see that there was an ample supply of firewood and that the fire was started and kept going for the cooking three times a day. Alice would carry water from the spring, go to the village store on her bike, and see that supplies of food were always on hand.

The camping trip started beautifully. The tent was put up; the broiler was set on some large stones a few paces away; and everything was OK for the start of a great vacation in the open spaces. There was a spring of clear, cold water just about a city block distant from their tent, which was pitched on a high point overlooking a lovely woodland. Alice brought a bucket of water for her mother to use in cooking and for everyone to drink. She found that the bucket got heavier with every step she took, but she arrived without even a spill. Carl found quite a bit of windfall wood nearby and soon had it chopped up into kindling and small logs and started the fire under the broiler. Mother always cooked a fine meal; and as the three sat out in the open, enjoying their supper and watching the colorful sunset, a whippoorwill's shrill call broke the stillness. Carl voiced everyone's sentiment: "This is the life!"

For two days this ideal life of freedom continued, and each enjoyed his special pleasure and faithfully carried out his job assignment. (I forgot to say that Mother's special pleasure was knitting, and she brought some yarn along.) But not many ideal situations last forever, and this one did not last beyond the second day. On the third day Carl forgot all about his part of the bargain. The very first day of their camping trip he had walked up the creek, quite a way, and had seen a large rainbow trout. He knew that a trout that had lived long enough to grow that large must be very wary and would take a lot of skill to catch. He determined to catch that granddaddy trout if it took a week. He decided to slip down to the deep hole where the trout was and watch its movements and find out what it was feeding on. Observing the movements of a trout and planning his capture is a fascinating experience, and Carl did not realize how long he had been away from camp until it began to get dark.

Alice was just as occupied with her special interest. She wandered off that third day, and each time she discovered a beautiful and unusual wild flower she would see another a little further away. She was having the time of her life, and the hours went racing by. She suddenly came to when she realized the sun had gone down.

Darkness puts a stop to most things we try to do in the out-of-doors, so both Carl and Alice started for camp. They were tired and hungry and thought, "How good it will be to sit down at the table and eat Mother's delicious supper." But there was no supper. The water jug was empty; there was no fire under the broiler and no wood in the woodbox; and poor Mother had been waiting all afternoon for her helpers to show up.

That day, a little after sunset, a boy and a girl learned a very important lesson about what freedom is.

41. Thanksgiving
THANKSGIVING DAY

Always and for everything giving thanks in the name of our Lord Jesus Christ to God the Father (Eph. 5:20).

It was Thanksgiving Day, and the whole family was gathered about the table. It was a big family, but just one look at the table would show that there was food enough for almost any family. Of course, a big turkey was there, with cranberries, mashed potatoes, hot rolls, a mincemeat pie, both tossed and molded salad—well, just about every kind of good thing to eat.

Mother suggested that they sing the Doxology and that then Grandfather would say the blessing. Bob was not sure what the Doxology was, but when Dad started the tune "Praise God from whom all blessings flow," he knew well enough. They sang like a good choir because everyone was happy and put their happiness into their voices.

Grandfather started his prayer as usual: "Almighty and all-loving God, our heavenly Father . . ." Then he thanked God for farmers who planted the seed, cultivated the soil, and harvested the grain. He thanked God for truckers who hauled the grain to the mill; for millers who ground the wheat into flour; for railroad engineers and trainmen who operated freight trains; for people who worked in canning factories; for wholesale grocers who gathered up vegetables and fruits from all over the country; for clerks who worked behind counters in grocery stores. In fact, Susan described that prayer pretty well when she said later: "Why, Granddad prayed all over the country!"

After dinner there was talk about our nation's foreign policy, about inflation and high prices, about the farmers who trade with Russia, and a lot of other matters. When she finally got a chance to make a remark, Susan turned to Grandfather and said: "Granddad, why did you give thanks for all those people we do not even know?"

That was what is called a leading question, and Grandfather was glad to answer it. "Well," said Grandfather, "I thought that at least once a year we ought to thank God for all the people who work for us all the time. You see, we had at least a thousand people helping us to have a good dinner today. They were working for us all over the country—in fact, all over the world."

Susan did not understand that statement. "Of course," she said, "We did not raise the turkey or grow the vegetables, but we got them all at Henry's market. I know, because I was with Mother when she went shopping."

"All right," said Grandfather, "Where did Mr. Henry get all those groceries?"

"I know the answer to that one," said Bob. "I play with Mr. Henry's son, George, and he told me his dad gets all his groceries at Associated Groceries on South Logan. In fact, I have been there with George."

"That is very interesting," said Grandfather. "I am wondering how many people Mr. Henry has running his farms, orchards, stockyards, and his mills and factories."

"Oh, now I see," said Bob. "Of course he buys vegetables, fruits, meats, and a lot of other things from people who raise them."

"I can see that," said Susan, "but Granddad mentioned people in other parts of the world. Mother did not go outside of town to get all these groceries."

"Susan," said Grandfather, "you know I am not much of a cook. However, I have some ideas about cooking. For instance, I imagine there were some spices in that mince pie. We also had quite a choice of drinks: cocoa, tea, milk, and coffee. In all my travels around these parts I have never seen a coffee tree, a cacao tree, or a tea bush." That helped get Grandfather's idea across.

That evening as the family sat around the fireplace, Susan and Bob said they believed this was the very best Thanksgiving Day they had ever had because they were thankful for so many people who had helped make it such a happy day.

42. A December Nightmare
CHRISTMAS EVE

If I had not come (John 15:22).

Johnny was very busy, but he was having fun and enjoying every minute. You see, it was just two weeks until Christmas, and a lot of activity was going on down at the church. Johnny was a member of the choir that was joining with the sanctuary choir to present the Christmas cantata. After the service the children were going caroling. Johnny was also to be one of the shepherds in the Christmas Eve program. Besides this, he had some personal plans for Christmas.

As the family sat at the dinner table Saturday night Johnny's father read the devotional and called attention to the text: "If I had not come" (the words of Jesus). "If Jesus had not come and there were no Christmas," said Father, "our family would not be so busy rushing around these days."

"Yes, and a lot of other things would be gone, too," said Mother. "For instance, we would not even have a church or a Christian religion."

That started a long discussion as each one thought how different the world would be if Jesus had not come. There would be no Christmas carols, anthems, greeting cards, pageants, Christmas trees, presents, school vacation . . . it was a long list.

When Johnny went to bed some time later he was still thinking what a terribly dismal world this would be if Jesus had not come. It seemed he had been asleep only a little while when he was rudely awakened. "Get up, you lazy boy! Get moving and get going!" Johnny rubbed his eyes and tried to wake up. He had never been awakened so rudely. He couldn't understand it. Neither his mother nor his father was in the room. He called to them, but got no answer. He dressed quickly and went downstairs. Dishes were on the table but no one was around. "I must have overslept," thought Johnny. "Mother and Daddy have gone to church. I must hurry down there as fast as I can." He ate a bowl of dry cereal and drank a glass of milk and started for the church.

As he went out the door he saw a gang of men working on a house across the street. They were making a lot of noise—pounding, sawing, throwing lumber around. He stepped across the street wondering why all the rush, why must they be working on Sunday. He asked one of the men, "Don't you know this is Sunday?"

The man looked at him and said, "Sunday? What is that?" Johnny felt he did not want to crack jokes with the fellow, for he was already late for church. He thought he would go down by the community Christmas tree on the way to church. As he approached the square he did not see the tree. A policeman was standing on the corner, and Johnny asked him if something had happened to the Christmas tree. "Christmas tree?" he said. "I am not very familiar with the name of trees. That one is an oak, and the one over there is an elm. I never heard of a Christmas tree."

"It's the tree with all the colored lights, and with the manger scene under it," said Johnny.

"A tree with lights and a manger scene under it?" said the policeman. "Son, are you all right?"

The way the policeman looked at Johnny caused him to think he had better be going on his way, so he started walking fast toward the church. When he got to the place where the church should be, he went right back on his heels. There was no building there at all, only a vacant lot. A signboard read FOR SALE in large letters, and the words "Good business site" were written on it.

What in the world could have happened? Johnny could see no signs of a fire or a windstorm. There was no debris around. There was no evidence that any building had ever been there.

While he was wondering about this, he decided to go by the YMCA and play around in the gym for a while. When he turned the corner at Lenawee and Townsend he saw another vacant lot. Some boys were playing football, and he watched them for a while. When he got a chance he asked them, "Where is the YMCA building?" "The YMCA—what is that?" they asked. "The Young Men's Christian Association, of course," said Johnny. "What is 'Christian' and what is 'association'?" they asked.

Johnny thought if they had never heard of the "Y" they certainly did not know what was going on in their own hometown, and he would not have time to explain it all this morning. He thought he would walk by some of the downtown shops on his way home and

110

look at the toys and gift suggestions in the windows. He saw tools, books, furniture, and clothing, but no toys, no Christmas decorations, no gift suggestions. He asked a man standing on the corner: "Where are all the toys and Christmas gifts?"

"Christmas gifts?" said the man. "I am a newcomer to this town and I have not heard about anything like that, so I am afraid I cannot be very helpful."

Johnny was really in a daze. Nothing was like it should be. Everything was wrong. He decided to get home just as fast as he could and find out what was going on. He started on the run and he must not have been watching where he was going, for all of a sudden he went *wham* into something—and that woke him up, for really he had been asleep and having a terrible nightmare.

He jumped out of bed and ran downstairs. His mother was preparing breakfast. She looked at him and said: "Johnny, are you awake? You look like you are walking in your sleep."

Johnny told her about the terrible dream he had had and said, "We really are going to have Christmas, aren't we?"

"Why, of course, Johnny," said Mother, "the biggest and the best we have ever had. Now you get upstairs and get ready for Sunday School and forget about that bad dream—hurry!"

Johnny went very slowly up the stairs. It was hard to get that horrible dream out of his mind. A little later when they were all at the breakfast table and Father asked Johnny to return thanks, he said: "Thank you, God, for your love; thank you for sending Jesus; thank you for Christmas." And he meant every word of that prayer.

43. The Jewelry Box
CHRISTMAS

Is not this the carpenter, the son of Mary? (Mark 6:3).

Bob was discouraged, weary, and sad. This was Christmas Eve, and he so much wanted to finish that jewelry box for his mother. There were things he might have bought for her, but he wanted to give his mother something he made himself. The jewelry box was a good idea, all right, but Bob just could not make the corners come out as they should. He had sawed the wood very carefully (it was fine walnut) and tried to fit the pieces together, but the joints simply were not right. They looked awkward and bulky, not neat and finished as they should be.

He decided to take a walk and think things over. Perhaps he would have to give up trying to complete the box for Christmas. He could give mother a greeting card with a note at the bottom saying there was a special present coming for her later. But that did not seem right either. He must try again and see if he could make those corners fit as they should. Father could help if he had the time, but he had been working late at the office every night. He was so tired when he got home that Bob did not think he should ask him to go down to the workshop.

As he walked along he noticed a man sitting on a bench in the park. He seemed young, but he had a beard. He had a very pleasant face and greeted Bob as he went by. Bob stopped to have a neighborly chat with him and noticed that there was a carpenter's tool box on the bench. It just occurred to Bob to talk to him about his box problem.

"Sir, are you a carpenter?" asked Bob. "Why, yes, I am," replied the stranger. "May I ask you one question?" said Bob. "Of course, ask as many as you like," said the stranger. So it happened that they got into quite a discussion about wood fitting, especially on corners. The stranger said: "From what you say, you probably need to miter those corners."

Bob did not know what mitering meant, and his puzzlement led to his inviting the stranger to his home to take a look at the unfinished box. As they walked along they talked about the Christmas season,

112

and Bob explained that he was making this box for his mother as a special present. He said he was very disappointed that he could not make it look as it should. He wanted it to be very special. The carpenter seemed to know exactly what the trouble was. He promised to give Bob some help, and Bob was certainly glad he had met up with a stranger who was a carpenter.

When Bob's new friend looked at the box, he praised Bob for his careful work of sanding the wood and polishing it off. He explained it was necessary to have a miter box in order to cut the exact angle needed for a mitered corner. It sounded so difficult that Bob was even more discouraged than ever. He thought perhaps he had tackled something beyond his ability. But the stranger was sure he could do it. He showed Bob how to make a miter box with three pieces of scrap wood and helped him cut some grooves at right angles. Then he held the wood while Bob sawed the corners. Really, it seemed easy with the carpenter helping. The corners fit perfectly, and the box was finished and polished before suppertime. It really was beautiful.

Mother called Bob to supper. She had heard him talking to someone in the workshop and suggested that he bring his friend to the table. The strange carpenter accepted Mother's invitation and thanked her for her kindness.

That supper was one the family will never forget—all because of the stranger Bob had found in the park. He was so interesting. He seemed to know so many things, and just to hear him tell a story was thrilling. He was so alive! Perhaps the right word is *radiant*. The family just felt as though they had known him all their lives, even though they had just met him. Well, it was hard to explain; but every member of the family insisted that he must spend the night with them and stay for Christmas Day. He did accept the invitation to spend the night, and after a delightful evening around the fireplace he went up to his room.

The next morning was Christmas, and there was a lot of excitement. After a while Bob remembered the stranger and went upstairs to thank him for his help with the box. He knocked on the door, but there was no answer. He opened the door and looked in. No one was in the room. The bed had not been slept in.

Bob rushed down to report to the family. He told them what a

113

wonderful teacher the mysterious carpenter was and how easy it was to work with the wood when he was helping. Then, all of a sudden, a thought flashed across his mind and shook Bob's whole being. Could the man possibly have been. . . . Yes, HE REALLY MUST HAVE BEEN!

44. A Girl at the Manger
CHRISTMAS

You will find a babe wrapped in swaddling cloths and lying in a manger (Luke 2:12).

Sarah was a bit nervous and very excited. You see, tonight she was to stay all night at the inn in Bethlehem. She had never spent the night away from home in her whole life. Being at the inn, however, was not as unusual as it might seem. Sarah's Uncle Nathan and Aunt Anna kept the Bethlehem Inn.

Sarah was not going as a guest but as a helper. Uncle Nathan was expecting a crowd of guests at the inn because of a decree the Roman emperor, Augustus Caesar, had made. He had decided that all the people in his empire must be taxed. In order to get a complete list of all these people, he demanded that each person go back to the town or city where he was born and register there with the town clerk.

Of course, quite a number of young people who had lived in Bethlehem had married and moved to other towns. Their parents still lived in the hometown, and they would stay with them when they came to be enrolled. But there were many families who once lived in Bethlehem who had moved away and had no relatives still living there. They must have rooms at the inn. Since there was only one inn or hotel in the town, it was easy to see that it would be rather crowded.

Uncle Nathan was the kind of man who made plans well in advance. He knew there would be too much work for his wife Anna to handle all by herself. He remembered his little niece, Sarah, and thought, *I just wonder if Sarah wouldn't like to come here and help her aunt.*

Uncle Nathan's guess was right, for Sarah was delighted. She could make beds, sweep, and scrub the floors; and she could cook some, too. Of course, most of her cooking had been candy and cookies, but she could follow directions. And at least she could carry pots and pans, wash dishes, and be handy around the kitchen. She just knew she would have a lot of fun with her Aunt Anna.

When Sarah arrived at the inn and was greeted by her uncle and aunt she was glad, but felt a bit strange too. But soon so many things

115

were happening and there was so much to do that she felt right at home. In fact, everyone around the place was busy every minute of that day. Abner, the gateman, Michael, the stable boy, and Sam, the general handyman, all had their hands full.

It was a long day, and by sundown all were ready for a rest. But just then, when Uncle Nathan was closing the gate for the night, a man and woman came up wanting a room. Uncle Nathan said: "Really, I am very sorry, but we do not have a single room left. All the rooms are taken."

Aunt Anna and Sarah heard them talking at the gate and came out to see who it was. The man looked very tired. He was leading a small donkey, and on the donkey sat a woman who appeared to be extremely weary. The man pleaded: "Please arrange a place for her. I can get along somehow, but she is very tired and must get some rest."

Nathan was about to say that there was no possible chance for a room when Sarah said: "She can have my room, Uncle Nathan. I can sleep on the floor in the hallway. I don't mind."

Aunt Anna said: "No, Sarah, you do not need to do that. We can surely arrange somehow. The poor woman must have a bed. How about the stable, Nathan? Couldn't we make a bed of straw there? It will be a shelter, and we could make her comfortable."

Since that was the best they could do, the bed was made in the stable; and the couple settled down for the night.

When Sarah got to bed it did not take her long to go to sleep, for she was really tired. But it seemed only a few minutes when she was awakened. Someone was pounding on the gate, and a dog was barking. Uncle Nathan was up at once, going to the gate, and Aunt Anna was right behind him. She feared it might be some of the ruffians who roamed around and caused trouble in the neighborhood.

Of course, Sarah could not stay behind. She slipped on her robe and tiptoed out toward the gate. To her surprise Uncle Nathan was opening the gate! Then several shepherds came in. One was carrying a lamb. All of them looked very excited. They were taking about something that had just happened. Suddenly one of them said: *"Look!* The *light!"*

They all looked. The light was coming from the stable. They walked slowly toward the bright glow; and as they reached the stable door, they saw an amazing sight. There in a manger was a tiny baby. The mother was bending over him. There was a wonderful radiance of light all around. It was not like the light of a candle or an oil lamp. It was a white light like that of the moon or a star. There was music in the air. A shepherd said, "Truly this is the Christ, the one the angels told us we would find!"

All fell to their knees. They felt a divine presence. Sarah had heard her father tell about the words of the prophets saying that God would send one who would save his people. She knew in her heart that this truly was that one. As she knelt before the manger and looked at the face of the tiny child, she said, in a whisper—but God could hear—"Holy Child, to you I give my heart, my life, my all—for now and for always!"

So it was that there was a girl at the manger that holy night. She learned the glorious meaning of Christmas, and all her life long, she never forgot.

45. Pretzels

Pray then like this (Matt. 6:9).

This is a "faraway" story. By that we mean it is faraway in time, having supposedly occurred about 150 years ago; faraway in distance, having probably taken place in Germany; and faraway from the truth—possibly—as it is a folktale and may or may not have ever happened.

So we will travel, in imagination, across the ocean to Germany and inquire about a monastery. This will be difficult to locate because we do not even know the name of the monastery. However, we will not try to visit all of them in the country. We will just use more of our imagination and decide in our own minds where it is located and what took place there about 150 years ago.

We have one lead: There was at least one monk, and probably several of them, who loved children and talked with them whenever opportunity offered. Perhaps there was a class of girls and boys who met in the monastery for instructions. They must have been awed by the high ceilings, the beautiful paintings on the walls, and the hundreds of beautifully bound books on the high shelves. They probably wondered about the many men walking about so quietly, all clothed in long brown robes tied with a cord around the waist. I'm sure they were very quiet and listened to every word as they sat in this solemn building or on the grass in the courtyard outside.

It must have been near Christmas when the incident we are thinking about occurred. The monks who taught the class of boys and girls got to discussing Christmas and the children. What could they give each child as a present? Of course, as you know, monks in a monastery have little or no money to spend on Christmas presents. They must consider something very simple and very cheap. Yet they wanted it to be attractive and nice.

It may be that candy was the first thing they talked about. Then they may have said: "Candy is nice, but children always get candy at Christmastime. We want to give them something quite different." Then they probably talked of various kinds of toys, but toys would be out of the question because they cost a lot of money. After a great deal of discussion perhaps one monk said: "Bread is often spoken of in the Bible. It is also considered man's most important food. Why not give them some kind of bread?" That, of course, caused a lot of discussion. Who would think of giving a loaf of bread, a bun, or even a sweet roll for a Christmas present?

However, it must have been finally agreed that they would give the children some kind of bread if they could figure a way to make the bread pretty, tasty, and attractive to the children. But how could that be done? A baker ought to be helpful, so a committee of the monks went to the village baker and put the problem to him. Could he bake some kind of bread that would taste good, be quite different, and be attractive to children?

Then we can imagine the baker standing on one foot and then the other, twiddling his nose, shaking his head, and looking at the ceiling. Then he asked some questions: "Do the children pray?" Of course. "Do they fold their arms when they pray?" As a matter of fact, they do. "Then watch what I can do with this piece of dough!"

He twisted the dough to look like arms folded in prayer, put grains of salt on it, baked it to make it shiny and crisp, and said, "Here you are, pretzels for prayers!"

Maybe it happened that way; maybe not; but who knows for sure?

46. Jesus Came Alive!

EASTER

And Joseph took the body, and wrapped it in a clean linen shroud, and laid it in his own new tomb, which he had hewn in the rock; and he rolled a great stone to the door of the tomb, and departed (Matt. 27:59–60).

You do not know me, so I will tell you who I am before I begin my story. I live in Arimathea and am the nephew of Joseph, whom you have heard about. He is a prominent Pharisee and a member of the Sanhedrin. He is the person who asked Pilate for the body of Jesus after Jesus was crucified. My uncle Joseph, with the help of Nicodemus, wrapped the body of Jesus in linen cloths and placed him in the tomb which my uncle had had hewn out of the solid rock.

Perhaps you have never seen a tomb like this. It is very difficult to carve a room out of solid rock, but this is the way my uncle's tomb was made. To close the entrance, a large round flat rock was cut and made to roll in a groove in the rock base. It was very heavy and took several men to move it. When it was rolled directly in front of the tomb, it closed the opening without leaving even a crack.

The story I am going to tell is an amazing one. After the body of Jesus was put in the tomb and the round rock rolled in front of the doorway, we all went home and were very sad. I suppose the disciples of Jesus felt sadder than anybody else. They had been with him for about three years and had grown to love him very much. Then, too, they believed that he was the Messiah the prophets had written about. They thought he would free our people from the Romans and set up our own government again. Now that hope was gone. But their sorrow was more than that. Jesus was the most wonderful person they had ever met. He cared so much for everyone. He cured the sick, made the crippled to be able to walk, caused the blind to be able to see, and helped everyone who was in trouble. He also preached the most interesting sermons about God and his love.

Now here is the unusual part. Early in the morning, just about three days after my uncle had put the body of Jesus in the tomb, two women, friends of Jesus, came to the tomb. They were going to put spices and ointment on the body of Jesus. They wondered how they would be able to move the heavy stone from the entrance, but when they came to the tomb they saw the stone already rolled away. Two strange men stood there, dressed in bright white robes. They told the women that Jesus was not in the tomb but that he had come alive again. That was surprising news. Then one of the women actually saw Jesus and talked with him. At first she thought he was the gardener, but when he called her name she knew that the man was really Jesus.

When the news got to the disciples of Jesus, two of them ran all the way to the tomb from town and saw that the tomb was empty. They spread the news all over town that Jesus had come alive. Several of the disciples of Jesus saw him before the day was over. Later they all gathered in an upstairs room to talk about this amazing thing that had happened and to pray. Jesus came right in where they were, though they had locked the door. You see, they were afraid of the police since the authorities had killed Jesus, their teacher.

Well, everybody knows about Jesus coming alive now, but I wanted to tell you what I knew about it because I was right there with my uncle when he and Nicodemus put the body of Jesus in the tomb. This was the saddest day of my life. The day I heard that Jesus had come alive again was the happiest day I have ever known. Everything became different then. We do not need to be afraid of the Romans anymore. We do not even need to fear to die, for Jesus changed all that. No wonder everyone who knows about Jesus coming alive wants to talk about it to everybody they meet. Could you think of anything more important than that?

47. The Easter Amaryllis
EASTER

Christ the Lord is risen today, Alleluia! (Easter hymn by Charles Wesley).

Marcie's fourth-grade class was studying botany in a very interesting way. They were planting all kinds of seeds, placing them in boxes on the window ledge, and making notes as they watched them grow. The most interesting of all their plants was an amaryllis bulb.

This bulb was black, or very dark brown, and was about the size of a baseball. Miss Armington had all the class read the instructions for planting. Then they took a medium-sized pot, put some peat moss in the bottom, and placed the big bulb on the peat moss with the pointed side up. They packed peat moss all around the bulb, leaving just a bit of the pointed part sticking out. According to the instructions, they were to pour water on the peat moss, soaking it thoroughly, and also put some water in the saucer under the pot.

The children did everything exactly according to directions. Then they began their long watch to see how it would grow and develop. It was to be kept at a temperature of seventy to seventy-five degrees. That was easily arranged, for the maintenance man would see that the room was kept warm.

The printed directions said that the amaryllis would not show any sign of life for probably a week or ten days. After a week they turned the pot around, looking at all sides; and they could not see any sign of life. They were disappointed and a bit worried. Miss Armington was sure that all was well and suggested that in a few more days things would begin to happen.

The teacher was right. On Monday when the children came back to school there was a definite narrow green line across one side of the top of the bulb. On the next day this green line was distinctly a growing something. Another green line was showing on the other side. Now the fun began. John was determined to see just how fast the bulb would grow, so he brought a yardstick to school and left it on the windowsill so it would be handy for measurements.

Those stems were so short and did not look at all like the long narrow leaves on the instruction sheet. They grew so slowly! But they

122

did grow every day. Those two green somethings pushed up and up, and after a while they were long, narrow fronds. Then the children noticed something else. The bulb was sending up some more green somethings. On either side of the fronds was another green something. These were not long and narrow but plump and pointed. They must be the beginnings of the blossoms!

And so they really were. Again, the progress was very slow. Then both buds and fronds began to shoot up rapidly. The fronds were now about eighteen inches tall and were beginning to bend over. Glen said he had just what was needed to prop them up straight. That afternoon he brought a round stick about two feet long. They stuck the stick in the peat moss, and Betty found a piece of white yarn that was just right to tie the fronds to the stick.

Now the plump, pointed buds grew so rapidly that the class could almost see them reach up. Nothing was ever watched as closely as were those buds. The children could not keep their eyes away from the window. When the children went home on Good Friday the blossoms had not yet come out, but there was a definite tint of pink showing through the green jacket. The blossoms were ready to pop out at any minute!

On Monday when the children came back to school, they could not wait to get into the room to look at their amaryllis. There it was in all its glory: not one, not two, but *four* beautiful trumpetlike blossoms, pointing in all directions!

Miss Armington had an idea for the Easter assignment. Each one was to write down what he or she thought the amaryllis was saying to them.

Marcie knew at once. She was sure the four beautiful blossoms were announcing to all the world—to the east, to the west, to the north, and to the south: "Christ the Lord is risen today, Alleluia!"

48. Baptized!
MISSIONS

Peter said to them, "Repent and be baptized every one of you in the name of Jesus Christ for the forgiveness of your sins" (Acts 2:38).

Wembo was deeply troubled. Kapita had brought him bad news. Yes, it must be bad news indeed. Kapita told him he had heard—not from Jati himself, but in a roundabout way—that Jati was to be baptized! It was a most peculiar story, for it seemed that Jati knew all about what was to happen to him; yet he was not one bit troubled about it. In fact, it was understood that plans were already completed to have Jati baptized in the river in just three days!

Now, that you may better understand this strange story, you must know that Wembo, Kapita, and Jati were all African boys who lived in the Belgian Congo in Equatorial Africa back in the jungle, in a small village not far from the Congo River. None of these boys had ever been any farther away from his village than he could walk in a day's time. None of them knew very much about the big world beyond the jungle and the Congo.

Some time ago a white man and his helpers had come to the village where these three boys lived and had told them some wonderful stories about the great spirit of the world. The things he told were interesting and so amazing they could hardly believe they were true. The fathers of Wembo and Kapita had gone to the village witch doctor and talked with him about the white teacher. He told them that the strange teachings were very dangerous and that fathers were not to allow their children to listen to the white teacher. He said if they did listen terrible things would happen to their family, even to the whole village. Evil spirits would swoop down and punish everyone who had listened.

Since the witch doctor had said this, neither Wembo nor Kapita had dared go near the white teacher. Jati must have gone, and now he was to be visited by the evil spirits because he had listened. To be baptized—what kind of punishment could that possibly be?

Wembo and Kapita asked questions of people who had been listening to the white teacher. They said he would come through the jungle from some distant place and teach for two or three days, then disappear and not be back until the moon was full again. These people said there was to be a "baptizing" in the river on the day they called Sunday, after the sun had risen to the top of the sky. Evidently this was the time when Jati was to be punished by being baptized. Wembo and Kapita were determined to be there and to protect him if any harm was threatened.

So on Sunday afternoon when a crowd of village people gathered on the banks of the little stream that runs down from the village to the Congo River, Wembo and Kapita were hiding behind trees in the jungle where they could watch every move that was made by the white teacher and his helpers. They could see Jati, together with several other boys and girls and their parents, sitting on the ground waiting to hear the white teacher.

The teacher rose and opened a black book. He read in a loud voice so all could hear: "We were buried therefore with him by baptism into death, so that as Christ was raised from the dead by the glory of the Father, we too might walk in newness of life" (Rom. 6:4).

"All these who are to be baptized this afternoon understand what that means," said the teacher. "I have talked with them about it. There may be some here who do not understand. Before our baptismal service, I wish to explain exactly what baptism means."

Then the teacher told about the great Teacher, Jesus, and his coming to earth because he was sent by God, who is our heavenly Father. He told how Jesus died on a cross, suffering terribly. He did it not because he was bad, but because he was sent by God to save men from their sins. Jesus took the blame for the sins of all people everywhere and suffered on the cross for all this sin. Everyone is a sinner and breaks God's laws, but God is all-loving and forgiving. If people return that love and ask God to forgive them, he will do it for the sake of Christ, who died for them.

When people's sins are forgiven and they have accepted Christ as their Savior, they begin living a new kind of life. It is the kind of life that pleases God and makes them truly children of God. As a picture of this new life, Jesus asked those who believe to be baptized. A great teacher of long ago, known as the apostle Paul, explained the meaning of baptism as being buried with Christ and raised again to newness of life. Just as we have put off the old selfish persons we

125

once were, so we are lowered into the water and immersed to picture burial of the old dead self. Then, just as we have begun a new life and are a new person through the wonderful power of Christ, so we are lifted up out of the water to symbolize that new person.

The teacher added: "Remember, it is not the water that makes you a Christian and a new person, but the giving of your heart and your whole life to God. The baptism is just a picture or object lesson to let others know your love for Christ as your Savior."

The teacher also said: "Let me remind you, too, that baptism is just the beginning. As a Christian you will 'walk in newness of life.' That means you will live every day and grow taller and stronger in the likeness of the Christ, whom you serve."

Wembo and Kapita watched in wonder. They had never heard such words. They had never seen such happy people. When they sang their faces shone with brightness. The boys watched Jati as he was baptized. After all was over they ran to Jati and said: "Jati, please take us to the teacher and ask him to baptize us too. We also want to be Christians and learn to be like the Jesus he talked about."

49. Coconut Missionaries
MISSIONS

So, every sound tree bears good fruit, but the bad tree bears evil fruit. Thus you will know them by their fruit (Matt. 7:17,20).

Tourists were driving along a Florida highway. They stopped to watch some workmen cutting coconuts from palm trees along the parkway. One of the workmen tossed them a couple of coconuts with his compliments. As they drove on their way, one of the tourists remarked: "The coconut is the great foreign missionary of the plant kingdom. There are many plants that send their seeds journeying on the wind or on the feet of animals and birds to distant places. But the coconut has traveled around the globe, planting its trees on every island and mainland of the tropical zone."

It is true. Coconut palm trees flourish along the ocean beach. When the fruit is ripe the big coconut pods drop off, and the tide often washes them off to sea. The nut itself is well protected inside a tough fibrous shell. This is watertight and floats off on the water. The wind blows it along, and it may travel hundreds of miles before it finally is washed up by an incoming tide. On the beach it will send out its roots and sprout. Soon a little palm tree is growing on that shore, many miles distant from the tree from which the coconut dropped.

As we look at a map of the world, we find the coconut palm growing in every country and on every island of the tropics. If you want an interesting theme for a study, take the missionary travels of the coconut and trace its journey around the world. As you look in the encyclopedia for the fruits grown in various countries, in the tropical zone you will easily trace the traveling coconut.

The coconut is not just a traveler on a fun trip. The new trees that are planted bear fruit and serve people in a score of useful ways. It is said that the coconut palm is one of the most useful of all trees. First, the nut itself. The coconut meat is not only good to eat, but the taste is delicious. What about a coconut cake or a sundae made with a ball of ice cream rolled in shredded coconut?

There is more food in a coconut than the shredded meat. The dried meat is called *copra*. Copra is a very important export from

127

countries that grow coconuts. The oil is pressed out of this dried coconut meat and used for making cooking fats, margarine, and soap. Some of it is also used for making candles.

Inside the coconut is a white liquid called coconut milk. The natives drink this milk, and it is also allowed to ferment and used as vinegar.

You need not throw away the hard shell of the coconut. It can be used as a bowl or cup. You can cut spoons from it, too. The outer fibrous husk that was torn off to get the nut out is not destroyed, either. It is very useful. It can be used for fertilizer and burned for fuel.

Both the trunk of the coconut tree and the leaves are useful. Most of you have seen palm leaf fans. For more skillful work the leaves are cut into strips—some very narrow and others wider—and woven into baskets, hats, chair seats, matting, handbags, and many other articles. Ropes are also made from the fiber.

If a workman in coconut palm country were building a house, he would probably build the house with splits from the trunk of the tree and then thatch the roof with the palm leaves.

Coconut palm trees grow to great heights, some reaching one hundred feet. They may produce fruit for thirty or forty years. The nuts grow in clusters of fifteen or twenty, and one must climb far up the trunk to pick the fruit.

Of course, no animal, bird, or plant could be a true missionary. A missionary is one who goes on a mission and carries a message. A Christian missionary carries the message of God's love, as shown in Christ, who died that all men might live eternally. But the coconut palm gives a good illustration of persistence, determination, and endurance under trying circumstances. It travels to the ends of the earth and bears good fruit that serves the needs of people faithfully through the years.

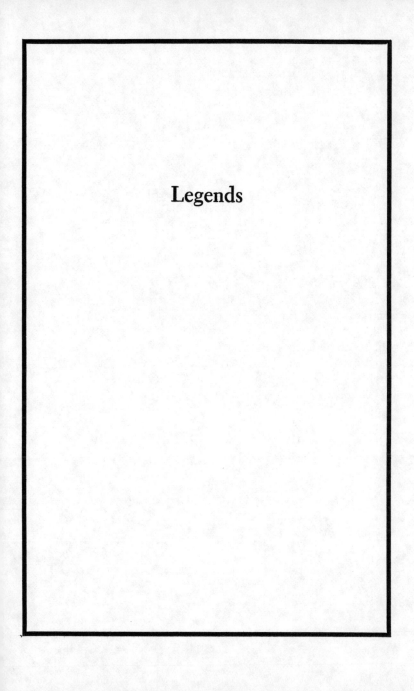

Legends

50. Johnny Appleseed

Whatever you do, in word or deed, do everything in the name of the Lord Jesus (Col. 3:17).

In the early days of our country, at the beginning of the 1800s when the pioneers were settling the West, there was a man in the Ohio Valley area known and loved by all and helpful to everyone he met. His name was John Chapman, but everyone knew him as "Johnny Appleseed." If you had met him you would have looked at him twice, for he was strangely dressed. He was barefoot, wore a gunny sack for a shirt with holes cut for his head and arms, and his crude trousers were held up by one leather thong across his shoulder from one side in the back to the other side in front. For a hat he often wore a tin saucepan. This was useful as a headpiece to protect him from low branches and to keep his head dry when it rained. It was also his utensil for cooking the simple food he ate: berries, wild fruits, roots, and food given him by friends. He never ate the flesh of bird or animal, for he would not kill a living thing. It might be said he loved everybody and everything that breathed.

To give practical expression to his love of people, Johnny Appleseed had a unique idea. He went about planting apple seeds. He got these seeds from the apple mash thrown out by cider mills in Pennsylvania. He wanted everyone wherever he traveled to enjoy sweet apples from his trees. Can you think of a better way to serve a multitude of people? Could you count the apples in any of the seeds he planted? Think of the trees that sprouted and grew, the thousands of bushels of apples that resulted, and the tens of thousands of people who must have enjoyed them. Apples are one of the best of foods. You can eat them raw as they come from the tree, cook them into pies or dumplings, or you can caramel them. It seems the ways to eat them are almost endless. Then too, they are a health food: "An apple a day keeps the doctor away."

Tradition reports that Johnny Appleseed would revisit the area where he had planted his apple trees, cultivate them, prune them, and cause them to produce more and better apples. He was also helpful to all the people he met. He made his living by mending pots, pans, and kettles; and he would accept whatever was given him for his work. He had no set price and was not concerned about money.

People enjoyed his stories and often invited him to eat a meal and to stay the night with them. He always carried his Bible and usually was asked to read to the family. He read while lying on the floor on his back. So you see that even in his reading he was himself, doing it his way. He also played a violin and would entertain with his music. Johnny Appleseed was a friend of everyone—white settlers, Indians, young and old, good and bad. He tried to do his part to build a brotherhood and peace among all people. He was a "one-man peace corps."

For forty-six years Johnny Appleseed went on his leisurely way up and down the land, planting apple seeds and seeds of kindness and scattering goodwill right and left. It would be impossible to begin to calculate the good this quiet, simple man did. His apple seeds are symbols. One apple seed that sprouts into a tree may produce a thousand bushels of apples over the years. No one could even imagine how many of the seeds from these apples sprouted into trees and continue the progression of helpful shade and fruit for all who came that way. In fact, even though Johnny Appleseed lived so long ago, the process of reproduction has surely continued his orchards until this present time and will project them far into the future.

So this is the story of what one kindly man did for his whole generation of fellowmen and their children and grandchildren. One day, after his usual tramp through the woods, tired and wet from the rain, he was invited to spend the night at the home of one of his many friends. As usual he told his stories, read from his Bible, and lay down for a well-earned rest. He went to sleep and did not wake up. In imagination we can picture his soul journeying on and on through the future, smiling at all he meets, and doing a good turn to every

132

fellow traveler. Then our imagination takes us beyond the earth to heaven, where God knows every good work that Johnny Appleseed ever did. We can hear the Master greeting him at the end of the day, "Well done, Johnny; come in and make yourself at home in your Father's house."

51. John Henry

By this we know love, that he laid down his life for us; and we ought to lay down our lives for the brethren (1 John 3:16).

As you drive east on route 12 in West Virginia, approaching the little town of Talcott, you are attracted by the sight of a red caboose standing on a widened roadside plot and the statue of a workman with a sledgehammer in his hand, bending over as if at work on the job. This is the memorial to the famous legendary steel driver known as John Henry. The caboose and monument are directly above the Big Bend tunnel on the Chesapeake and Ohio Railroad, and the elevation gives a beautiful view of the Greenbrier River Valley.

What about John Henry? Of course, when legends are woven about a person it is difficult to know the real facts; but there would have been no legend had this man not been a man of real worth. It seems that the background of the story was a contest between a strong man and a steam hammer. Just about the time the long curving tunnel was being constructed (it is one mile long), a steam drill was invented and was to be tested in this tunnel. During those days—the tunnel was built between 1870 and 1873—digging was done by driving spikes into the solid rock with sledgehammers weighing ten pounds or more. The spikes made holes into which dynamite was placed to knock down the rock. Driving a spike into solid stone was in itself a very difficult job. It took both a lot of strength and a lot of determination. It was very exhausting work.

The introduction of the steam hammer was similar to the introduction of machinery into other kinds of work customarily done by hand. It meant that if the machine succeeded in doing the work and doing it better, the skill and strength of man would no longer be appreciated or needed. This is why the contest arose between the steam hammer and John Henry, the mightiest of the steel drivers. In his determination to beat the steam hammer, John Henry took two sledgehammers, each weighing twenty pounds, and determined to drive spikes with both hammers at the same time. Tradition says he won the contest, drilling two seven-foot holes in thirty-five minutes, while the steam drill bored

134

only one hole nine feet deep. But the tragedy of the event was that John Henry burst a blood vessel during his super effort and died after winning the contest.

Of course, this contest and his victory there did not make him a fabulous hero. What did was his day-by-day life with his fellow workmen and his attitude of concern for them and his helpfulness in many acts both great and small. We do not have a detailed list of these, but they must have been considerable. He must have helped a great number of people because after his death they wove all kinds of stories of his great and good deeds. It has been said that John Henry became for the construction industry what Paul Bunyan was for the lumber business. He was a hero not only of the railroad construction work, but of all types of gang labor.

Legend says that John Henry's actual features can be seen carved in the rock inside the tunnel, by unknown miraculous powers. It is also said that if one listens he can hear John Henry's ghost hammer still ringing deep down in the tunnel. Legend even created a different explanation of his death, saying that John Henry, hearing the dreaded sound of crumbling rock and knowing that a cave-in was approaching down the tunnel, stood with his broad shoulders against the heavy rock and held it back until his fellow workers could escape to the outside, though he died in the crash that followed.

The statue was erected by the citizens of the neighboring towns, calling themselves the Ruritan Club. The inscription concludes with the prayer: "May God grant that we always respect the great and the strong and be of service to others."

52. Casey Jones

Before automobiles were so numerous, people traveled a lot by train. The railroad was very popular, and many stories were told about the engineers, firemen, brakemen, and others who operated the system. One of the most famous of the engineers was Casey Jones. Many songs and ballads were written about him. When railroad people got together they sang his praise.

Casey was not his real name. He was christened John Luther Jones and was born in Cayce, Kentucky. There were so many John and Luther Joneses that John Luther soon came to be called Casey because of his birthplace. The name of the town was spelled C-a-y-c-e but pronounced the same as Casey.

Casey was a big fellow, six feet, four and a half inches tall, and the kind of person everyone liked. It was said that his heart was as big as his body, and he was good-natured all over. The fireman who worked with him every day "worshiped the ground he walked on."

It was the custom of the railroad company to assign a locomotive to an engineer as his personal responsibility, and he came to think of his locomotive as his own. He soon learned how to get the best results out of his engine. Casey knew all the moods of engine #382. He could work it up to a tremendous speed by taking advantage of grades and could make better time than most of the other engineers. He prided himself on always being on schedule. Time was often lost taking on water at the tank stations. Casey knew just how far his locomotive could go on a full tank of water, and he calculated so closely that he lost little time stopping at water stations. He was so skillful in his timing, picking up speed and slowing down for crossings, that he became famous among railroad folk as the greatest engineer on the road.

Engineers had special whistles on their locomotives, and each engineer could be recognized by the sound of his whistle. Casey's whistle had six pipes giving out sounds from low pitch to high, and he could play a tune on it—almost! He had a way of blowing that whistle that was all his own. He would start with a low croon, build up to a loud blast, and let it die out with a whisper. People all along the Illinois Central Railroad recognized that sound. As Casey went through town in the middle of the night, his friends would hear that whistle and say, "There goes good ole Casey!"

Casey Jones had started working for the railroad when he was sixteen, and after many years of apprenticeship he was allowed to "pull" a freight train. In his later years he was the proud engineer of the "Cannonball Express," the crack passenger train of the Illinois Central Railroad, running between Chicago and New Orleans. People of all ages soon came to know Casey. They loved him, watched his train go through town, and listened for his famous whistle.

April 30, 1900 was a fateful day in the life of Casey Jones. Having completed his run from Chicago to Memphis, Tennessee, he heard that the engineer who took the train from there to New Orleans was sick. Casey volunteered to continue the trip and substitute for his fellow engineer. So he climbed back into the cabin of his beloved engine #382 and pulled out of the station, headed for New Orleans.

Everything went smoothly as he sped through the night until he approached Vaughn, Mississippi. The weather had been rainy and foggy, but Casey was in the best of spirits; and the locomotive was moving beautifully. As Casey expressed it, "The old girl's got her high-heeled slippers on tonight!" For Casey's part all was perfect, but the rails were not clear. Three freight trains down the line were slow in pulling out of the right-of-way. One freight left the caboose protruding across the rails where Casey's "Cannonball" was coming at full speed ahead.

Tragedy was inevitable. As the Cannonball came around a double curve just outside of Vaughn, Casey suddenly saw the bright red lights of the freight. He yelled to his fireman—"Jump, Sim!" He applied the brakes and put the throttle into reverse, but it was too late. Casey saved the lives of his passengers, but he lost his own. When they found him in the wreckage he had one hand on the air brake and the other on the throttle.

Casey's death was mourned by people all over the country, and a Negro fellow worker wrote a song about his hero. It instantly became popular and was sung by railroaders up and down the line. It began:

"Casey Jones mounted to the cabin, Casey Jones, orders in his hand." It ended, "Casey Jones, bravest of the engineers." Yes, there have been many railroad men who gave their lives in their line of duty; but Casey Jones represents them all as a man dedicated to his task and ready to die for his fellowmen.

53. Paul Bunyan

With men this is impossible, but with God all things are possible (Matt. 19:26).

We have written about Casey Jones of railroad legend and John Henry, who was the hero of the steel drivers. We should not omit Paul Bunyan, the giant lumberman, who probably was the greatest mythological figure of them all. John Henry and Casey Jones were actual people, while Paul Bunyan was probably a dreamed-up conglomerate of all the spectacular characters who appeared in the lumber camps of Michigan, Wisconsin, and Minnesota and beyond in the early days of the great movement called "The Winning of the West."

All kinds of impossible stories have been woven around this amazing character, and stories continue to be concocted and told about his spectacular feats. It would be impossible to condense in one brief account an adequate story picture of this fabulous giant. As I remember it, he first came into view in the winter of the "blue snow." He had an ox that he called Babe. He measured Babe by the distance between his horns, which, it was said, was forty-two ax handles and a plug of chewing tobacco. His hooves must have been enormous because his tracks made the Great Lakes when they filled with rainwater. Babe was "twice as big as all outdoors and playful as a hurricane."

To give an idea of the tremendous strength of Babe, this amazing incident was told. The trace straps used to hitch Babe to the lumber sled were made of strips of rawhide. When Babe was to haul a whole forest load of lumber into camp, advantage was taken of the weather. When the rawhide was wet it would stretch to great lengths; when dry it would shrink. Babe would often arrive in camp around noon, but the stretching action of the wet rawhide would leave the load of lumber back in the woods. Then the sun would dry out the rawhide, and the shrinking action would bring the sled into camp long before supper time.

Paul himself was a giant of a man and capable of incredible feats of strength. When cutting lumber in the forest he customarily used two heavy axes weighing from fifty to seventy-five pounds. He swung both axes at the same time and made a complete circle turn, with the result that one slash of Paul's axes would fell from fifty to one hundred trees.

Paul did everything on a big scale. When his cook fried pancakes it took several men skating with slabs of bacon on their feet to grease the skillet. Then the pancakes were brought to the tables from the cook house on fast conveyor belts.

Attempts have been made to learn where the Paul Bunyan stories originated. Some maintain that they started among the loggers of Quebec and northern Ontario, with contributions from Norway, Sweden, and other forest areas of the old country. Others insist that Indian legends formed part of the stories, and still others believe that it all started in the forests of the Northwest country of the United States. At any rate, the stories are interesting and so fabulous as to stretch the imagination almost to the breaking point. In fact, since more stories are still being added to the list, anyone who has a whopping big impossible idea is welcome to add his tale to the mountain-high accumulation of tall tales.

But why include the Paul Bunyan legend in such a collection of stories as the present? Simply this: It is human nature to think big—or it really should be. And it is good for all of us to dream and project ideas far beyond the realm of the easily possible. We should always be thinking and believing clear beyond the horizon of the accomplished. It has been true that dreamers have been laughed at through the years, and persons who had unusual ideas of projects unheard of and considered unattainable have been labeled as queer. However, if there had been no way-out ideas in the minds of the pioneers and inventors, civilization would never have advanced. People laughed at Fulton and his steamboat and at the Wright brothers with their flying machine, but we know what happened in spite of the jibes and the pessimism. The whole amazing achievement in the world of space is even now fantastic and seemingly unbelievable, but it is a matter of proven fact. And it all started with dreams of the fabulously incredible.